the series on school reform

Patricia A. Wasley
University of Washington

Ann Lieberman
NCREST

Joseph P. McDonald
New York University

SERIES EDITORS

(Continued)

D0757199

the series on school reform, *continued*

This series also incorporates earlier titles in the Professional Development and Practice Series

Standards
of
Mind and Heart

CREATING THE GOOD HIGH SCHOOL

PEGGY SILVA
ROBERT A. MACKIN
Foreword by Tony Wagner

Teachers College, Columbia University
New York and London

Published by Teachers College Press, 1234 Amsterdam Avenue, New York, NY 10027

Library of Congress Cataloging-in-Publication Data

Silva, Peggy.
    Standards of mind and heart : creating the good high school / Peggy Silva, Robert A. Mackin ; foreword by Tony Wagner.
      p. cm. — (The series on school reform)
    ISBN 0-8077-4213-9 (cloth : alk. paper)—ISBN 0-8077-4212-0 (pbk. : alk. paper)
    1. School improvement programs—New Hampshire—Amherst—Case studies. 2. High schools—New Hampshire—Amherst—Administration—Case studies. 3. Souhegan High School (Amherst, N.H.) I. Mackin, Robert A. II. Title. III. Series.
LB2822.83.N49 S55 2002
373.742'8—dc21   2001055687

ISBN 0-8077-4212-0 (paper)
ISBN 0-8077-4213-9 (cloth)

Printed on acid-free paper
Manufactured in the United States of America

09 08 07 06 05 04 03   8 7 6 5 4 3 2

To Dr. Richard A. Lalley
who saw the future

To the residents of Amherst and Mont Vernon
who built the future

To the students of Souhegan High School
who are the future

Contents

Foreword

In this book, Peggy and Bob tell an extraordinary story of the creation of a new high school that truly aspires to educate all students to high standards—standards for the heart, as well as for the mind; standards for citizenship, as well as for future adult work. We can learn a great deal from their story about what is required to transform secondary education—the replicable principles and practices that make for a truly excellent public school.

For the first two years of Souhegan's existence, I was the school's "critical friend" and supervisor of teams of teacher interns from the University of New Hampshire. So I had an unusual vantage point from which to view the creation of a school from scratch. I listened in on faculty meetings from the very first day; I was constantly in and out of classes as I observed my teaching interns; I had private talks with Bob and others that often went long into the night.

Peggy and Bob will be surprised to hear this, but as I reflect back on that time and now read this account of their work, I am most struck by what we can learn from Souhegan about more effective systems of accountability in education.

Public education "accountability" is an abiding preoccupation of policy makers and business leaders today, and for some good reasons. Chief among them is the need to ensure that we are truly educating *all* students for a future that is very different from the one their parents were prepared for. Gone forever are the days when a ninth-grade level of education suffices as preparation for both work and citizenship. The knowledge economy and a more globalized society demand much more sophisticated skills for full participation. Lacking these, many poor and minority students will be left further and further behind economically, and will remain second class citizens with little or no voice.

Thus far, policy makers have addressed the accountability problem by mandating a series of new multiple choice tests that must be passed in order to graduate from high school or move from one grade level to the next. Even in those states that do not have such high expectations for students, test scores are often used to grade or rank schools, and there are serious political and social consequences for those schools that find themselves ranked below "average."

The problem with this approach, many educators claim, is that these machine-scored tests do not measure the sophisticated skills of critical thinking, problem-solving, and so on that are being emphasized increasingly in the classroom. The tests are also a one-time event that often do not give an accurate picture of an individual student's strengths and weaknesses, and for a variety of reasons the results often cannot be used to diagnose educational needs. Finally, the greatly increased emphasis on high-stakes testing threatens to drive curiosity and love of learning as motivations for mastery right out of the classroom. There's too little time and too much fear for such "leisure" pursuits.

But what is the alternative? Thus far, progressive educators have pleaded for "waivers" from the tests, rather than offering up an architecture for an accountability system that will measure the skills most needed and create positive motivations for learning and teaching.

Here is where we can learn some valuable lessons from the Souhegan story. Souhegan teachers paid attention to the standardized test results, such as the SATs, which many of their students took. But fundamentally, the school created a real alternative to "compliance-driven" accountability. They developed what I propose to call "relational accountability."

The decision to build a new school was an opportunity for the Amherst community to re-think the purposes of education and to develop a clear mission for their new high school. Students, teachers, parents, and the community spent endless hours discussing and finally coming to agreement on the goals of the new school. The creation of a focused, clearly articulated, and widely understood shared sense of purpose is the first requirement of a relational accountability system.

Furthermore, by its small size, by the organization of its faculty into teams and cross-disciplinary divisions, and by how time was spent with both the faculty and the community, the school fostered the development of relationships that were very different from those that characterize most high schools today. Teachers came to know their students well—their interests, strengths, and weaknesses as learners. Knowing students deeply, teachers were far more able to coach, nurture, and demand excellence from each student. Parents' and students' questions and concerns were actively welcomed and listened to with great care.

In the first year, Bob and the teachers heard that many parents were concerned about how the graduates of this new and very different high school would fare in the college admissions process. So they invited admissions staff from several leading New England colleges to talk and answer questions at the first Parents' Night. And in the second year of the school, I was asked to conduct a series of focus groups with some of the most able students and their parents so that the school might better understand and respond to concerns about heterogeneous grouping and fears of lack of sufficient academic challenge in the de-tracked school. Rarely do schools take the time to listen to its "customers" in this way. This ongoing dialogue and transparency is an essential element of "relational accountability."

But it was in the very way in which teachers worked together that we find the heart of the relational accountability system at Souhegan. In the overwhelming majority of schools in America, teachers work in isolation. They are, for the most part, insulated from the demands of parents and the community, and they work alone in their classrooms all day long. Faculty meetings are usually little more than brief monthly occasions for announcements and other forms of administrivia. It might even be said that a majority of older teachers see education as one of the last places in our society where one can be "self-employed." Once you close the classroom door, you are king or queen for the day.

Not so at Souhegan. Here, teachers spent long hours together discussing the curriculum and student work. They were constantly in and out of one another's classrooms. Many classes were team taught. Large and small group meetings of faculty were a time for true collaborative inquiry and problem-solving. Their relentless focus on improving teaching led them to reach out to others affiliated with the Coalition of Essential Schools, inviting them to visit the school to help assess the quality of student work, teaching, and curriculum.

The highly collaborative Souhegan approach to improving teaching and learning is a close cousin of the Japanese secret ingredient for improving schools. In their book, *The Teaching Gap* (New York: The Free Press, 1999), Stigler and Hiebert describe the way teams of Japanese teachers study a common learning problem shared by many of their students and collaboratively devise, test, and refine a series of lessons aimed at helping students learn more effectively. In Japan, as at Souhegan, this collaborative inquiry led to significant improvements in teaching and learning.

Another outstanding educator, Anthony Alvarado, puts the challenge more succinctly. When he was Superintendent of New York City's Community District Two, which is noted for its extraordinary success in raising the achievement levels of the most at-risk students under his leadership, Tony had a motto: "Isolation is the enemy of improvement."

More high stakes testing will not improve teaching and learning. Teachers, working alone, attempting to respond to ever changing district mandates, will never solve the twin challenges of education in the 21st century: How to teach new skills and how to motivate *all* students to aspire to achieve higher standards. Only by working together and in close collaboration with parents and the community will educators find new and better methods of teaching and motivating excellence. It is in this shared sense of purpose and the deeper relationships between teachers and students, among teachers, and with the school community that true accountability resides. This may be one of the most important lessons the Souhegan story has to teach us.

Tony Wagner

Acknowledgments

We want to recognize an extraordinarily powerful set of thinkers and practitioners who shed themselves of the vestiges of "old think" and embraced the possibilities of a new beginning. Our sincere thanks to Superintendent Dr. Richard Lalley, Assistant Superintendent Michael Galan, and our original Planning Team—Cleve Penberthy, Dan Bisaccio, Allison Rowe, Kim Carter, and Nancy Baker.

We were also blessed by a wonderfully supportive school board who understood that schooling for the 21st century needed a new vision. Thank you, May Balsama, Bill Donovan, Addie Hutchison, Ann Logan, Bob Kent, Bruce Ribolini, and Martha Christensen.

Ted Sizer's inspiration for creating a school where students would learn to "use their minds well" became an integral part of our vision. We appreciated his support and his frequent visits.

We are grateful to the residents of Amherst and Mont Vernon who supported the creation of the high school and who continue to support our students' efforts and achievements.

We are grateful to our editors Susan Liddicoat, Catherine Bernard, and Karl Nyberg, whose advice strengthened and streamlined our writing.

We each also want to recognize the individuals who have contributed to our lives and work:

Bob: The role as founding principal of Souhegan High School would never have occurred without the loyalty and support of my wife, Eileen. A lifetime New Yorker, she was willing to emigrate to the wilderness of New Hampshire to create a new home and a new life. Throughout the birth and rapid growth of Souhegan, she was there to provide encouragement to me and my colleagues and ultimately to become a respected member of the school community herself. For this, I will be forever grateful.

Peggy: I am grateful for the constant cheerleaders in my life: husband John, daughters Meghan and Kerry, sister Colleen, friend Carol Brennan, and the strong network of friends who have shared a lifetime of laughter with me. My writing voice was shaped by my mentors at the University of

New Hampshire Summer Writing Program, Dr. Fred Robinson, and writing fellows of the National Endowment for the Humanities Summer Program at the University of San Diego, Grace McEntee, and my writing partners in Educators Writing for Change.

It has been an honor to serve as Souhegan's first storyteller.

Introduction

In his address to the annual conference of the Coalition of Essential Schools, in November 2000, Cornel West, Professor of Religion and Afro-American Studies at Harvard University, passionately decried the loss of democratic engagement on the part of America's young people. He expressed fear that their reduced interest and involvement in America's governance would seriously threaten our future well-being as a free and healthy democratic society. He went on to remind the educators present that "undemocratic means voicelessness" and that we must take on a renewed commitment to democratizing our schools as one means of reenergizing student engagement.

For us, West's comments hit a dissonant chord. On the one hand, his assessment is disheartening. On the other hand, it gives added purpose to this book. It reminds us once again that in America's high schools we are experts at stilling the voices of our children. And in doing so, we foster student uninterest and disenchantment with the processes of democracy.

Next to prisons, high schools are the least democratic institutions in our American society. They are cursed by a tradition of hypocrisy—teaching and espousing democratic doctrine within the classroom, but doing it in a highly controlled, authoritarian manner that makes the actual practice of democratic principles largely nonexistent anywhere in the school. While it is okay to talk about empowering the American voter in a civics or an American history class, please don't bother schools with concerns about empowering students to make real decisions. Sure, kids can choose when and where the prom will be held, but don't ask them to evaluate their teachers or to make decisions about the implementation of a newly proposed block schedule.

It is this context that serves as impetus for our writing. While this is a book about a school, more than anything it is a book about democracy. It is a book that tells the story of how one new high school in New Hampshire aspired to foster the kinds of skills, attitudes, and behaviors in young people that lead to a more thoughtful and engaged citizenry. It describes a new set of high school practices and approaches that seek to give students the confidence to work together collaboratively, to express themselves with clarity and passion, to look beyond their own egos to a larger social order.

1

In other words, it is about a school that aspires to nurture young people to take their role in our democracy seriously.

The success of democracy requires a balance between intellectual and emotional expression—the ability of democratic citizens to think critically and to question, but to do so within a context of compassion, caring, and respect for others. This book, then, is also about personalization, about creating an environment where every student counts. Souhegan High School was designed with this premise in mind—an overriding belief that a school should be holistic in its commitment to develop the mind, body, and heart of all its students.

Opened in 1992, Souhegan High School reflects the best thinking of the secondary school reform literature. In part, the research says that most high schools are large, anonymous, and impersonal places where students come to be passive and uninterested in learning. High schools are often places where cliques of students openly reject the values of their peers—and are allowed to do so by virtue of the lack of intervention by the school. Consequently, students learn lessons of disrespect, self-absorption, mean-spiritedness, and distrust. High schools very often nurture competition rather than collaboration. Most importantly, most high schools do not foster thinking. Instead they value covering content at all costs, particularly at the expense of deeper understanding and of students' learning to use their minds well.

A DEMOCRATIC SCHOOL

Souhegan chooses to be different. At its core, Souhegan views democratic schooling as meaning that all students could learn basic knowledge and skills to a level of clearly stated proficiency. This belief leads to a commitment to heterogeneous grouping of students and to special education inclusion throughout the school. Students are encouraged to question both within their classrooms and within the larger context of the school.

The principal models an open-door policy and invites students to visit, particularly if they feel that the mission of the school is being abused. Annual community meetings of the entire faculty and student body ensure that democratic principles are being addressed.

The mission of the school is at the heart of our democracy and drives every aspect of the program. It is studied by students in the same way as the founding documents of the United States are studied in American history classes. A Community Council consisting of 25 students and 20 adults gives real voice to students in all major policy areas—an absolute reflection of the trust we hold in our young people. Our democratic school is more than lip service and pretense; it is the essence of the school's culture.

A PERSONALIZED SCHOOL

The other major tenet of Souhegan High School is a belief that every student counts, that no student should fall through the cracks that invariably exist in most schools. In 1992, our town looked at the disconnects between adolescents and adults and set out to create a personalized learning environment for our high school students.

We believed then, and we believe even more strongly today, that personalization offers a means of embracing students in the academic process, of capturing their hearts and their feelings as a means of engaging their minds. Creating human connections becomes the vehicle for opening up the intellectual engagement of our young people.

This book testifies to the importance and power of that process. We will demonstrate the life of a school in which all students feel a stake in the institution. We will magnify the voices within a real high school with real challenges. As school practitioners, we are the living research, the change process personalized, the primary sources for those who sit off-stage and prompt our work. We do not often see ourselves mirrored on the bookshelves of reform; the practitioner voice is too often missing from the conversation of how to prepare our students for their work in the 21st century. Through our responses to the particular needs of our students, we hope to inform, but more than that, we hope to inspire—public education offers far too little inspiration.

We have been continually inspired by others, and we are especially grateful for the work of Ted Sizer, Debbie Meier, Ernest Boyer, Arthur Powell, Michael Fullan, Phillip Schlecty, Robert Fried, Tony Wagner, Peter Senge, Robert Evans, Thomas Sergiovanni, Patricia Wasley, Mark Tucker, and Judy Codding.

Likewise, our larger Souhegan family has remained a constant source of inspiration for us. It is through their collective voices—our students, our teachers, our parents—that we will share the experiences that resulted from our conscious decision to create a new system of interpersonal relationships that, in turn, would form a learning community.

HOW THIS BOOK CAN MAKE A DIFFERENCE

Since the opening of Souhegan High School in 1992, the national energy around the reform and redesign of American high schools has increased dramatically. Ted Sizer's picture of the inertia-bound and intellectually impoverished high school so passionately portrayed in *Horace's Compromise* in 1984 seemed to unleash a torrent of criticism. Numerous reports and recommendations accompanied by new programs and federal funding emerged in the late 1980s and accelerated into the 1990s. The "shopping mall high school," once so widely esteemed, was now being viewed as the downfall of American secondary education—a huge, impersonal, and passive setting that spawned little student engagement and even less serious thinking.

In 1996, high school principals finally put themselves on the map with a landmark report that has since served as a widely quoted and highly regarded blueprint for change. *Breaking Ranks; Changing an American Institution* (1996) outlines the origins of our American high school of today and the programs and attributes that had come to fail us. Among the 82 powerful recommendations, the report stresses, first and foremost, the need to provide a personalized, student-centered environment. The report asserts, convincingly, that the very survival of our democracy is at stake if significant systemic change does not occur.

Shortly after *Breaking Ranks* was released, the U.S. Department of Education undertook a major funding effort to encourage the development of school reform models at every grade level. Not surprisingly, most of the models that emerged focused on elementary and middle schools, a reflection perhaps of the impermeability of high schools to change, or maybe the unwillingness of many reformers to work with such a highly evolved system of resistance as the high schools represented. Nevertheless, the Comprehensive School Reform Demonstration (CSRD) monies served to encourage serious efforts at high school change from a variety of places.

Examples of these models include the Coalition of Essential Schools (founded by Dr. Ted Sizer), a loosely structured design with a set of Common Principles calling for a focus on students' using their minds well, common academic standards for all students, a less-is-more curricular philosophy, and teachers acting as coaches/students as workers. At the other end of the spectrum, the Talent Development High School model out of John Hopkins University and others like it propose small learning communities—teams and academies—as the heart of their design. America's Choice high schools, a model designed by the National Commission on Education and the Economy, is built upon the "new standards" and includes a rigorous set of performance standards and an accompanying curriculum that they have been devising since 1989.

In 1997, the U.S. Department of Education (USDOE) undertook its New American High Schools project based on 12 key reform strategies that have proven, through research, to be effective in improving student academic performance. Between 1997 and 2001, USDOE selected about 50 high schools as exemplars of these reform practices. This undertaking, along with the federal funding provided for districts to engage in comprehensive school reform, has prompted increased interest in high school redesign work nationally.

Interestingly, the design of Souhegan High School in 1991 preceded this curve. Souhegan has become a model *Breaking Ranks* school; a reflection of the attributes of the America's Choice program and of Talent Development; an exemplar of the practices of the New American High School. Between 1997 and 2001, three brand-new high schools opened in other New England communities and each first studied and then modeled itself after Souhegan.

Frankly, this isn't such a strange phenomenon. Most of the national models and major research reports represent a high degree of commonality. For example, during a recent Summit Conference for High Schools in Rhode Island, the following themes and practices were identified as essential in any genuine high school redesign.

1. High standards are expected of all students.
2. Curriculum is richer, deeper, and more challenging for all students.
3. Instruction engages all students.
4. Assessment approaches, both classroom and schoolwide, are performance-based.
5. Schools are organized into small, highly personalized, and safe learning communities.
6. Adult advocates/mentors and personal learning plans are provided to/expected of all students.
7. Periods of instructional time are longer and more flexible.
8. Teacher collaboration and reflection on student work and teaching practice are evident daily.
9. Technology is integrated to provide improved instruction and opportunities for all students to gain computer and other technical skills.
10. School-to-career experiences through workplace/real-life learning are expected of all students.
11. Professional development of teachers is intensive, school-based, and focused on important teaching and learning issues.
12. Active alliances are built between schools and parents, employers, community members, and policy makers to promote student learning and ensure accountability for results.
13. Student assessment and program evaluation data are collected and analyzed regularly for purposes of school improvement.
14. Strong partnerships and articulation agreements are forged with higher education institutions.
15. Preservice education of teachers and the leadership development of principals are aligned with high school reform needs and initiatives.

Examining these themes in light of the practices demonstrated at Souhegan High School underscores the importance of its pioneering efforts. Unfortunately, most of the New American High Schools—the schools identified by the "Feds" to serve as exemplars for other high schools to replicate— are not typical, full-sized high schools. While they are excellent programs, they are usually smaller in size and often specialized in their focus (the Fenway School in Boston, with 250 students; the Marine Academy for Science and Technology in New Jersey, with 100 students). Souhegan High School, with 1,000 students, stands as proof that a "real" high school, the only high school in town, located in a typical American community, can serve as a model for others to emulate. Hopefully, in reading further, you will concur.

WHAT THIS BOOK IS NOT ABOUT

While there is much educational literature about innovative curriculum and instruction, and new approaches to assessment, this book is not one of them. Certainly we touch on these areas, but our primary focus is on the creation of a school that by virtue of its focus on democracy and personalization creates new standards and embraces and fosters more engaging forms of teaching and learning. In doing so, we have very consciously shaped and refined the academic aspects of our school to reflect the research of the past 20 years. For example, our curriculum

- Emphasizes depth over breadth
- Attempts to be integrated and interdisciplinary
- Offers honors challenges to all students within mixed-ability grouping
- Is highly constructivist and project-based
- Minimizes electives
- Teams students at grades 9 and 10

Our instruction

- Calls for teachers to be coaches, not sages
- Engages students to apply their learning
- Integrates technology into the classroom
- Calls for teacher collaboration and regular reflection

Our assessment

- Calls for performance-based approaches
- Revolves around rubrics and clear expectations of students

- Seeks major student exhibitions of learning
- Involves students in the design of assessment approaches

We have chosen, however, not to write in depth about these practices. Perhaps they will be the subject of our next book.

THE PURPOSE OF OUR WORK

An early reader of the manuscript lambasted the "celebratory" nature of our writing. She knew from her own experience that high school reform was often a wasteland of shattered spirits and palace intrigue, surrounded by a sea of tension. Convinced of the truth of her experience, she could not accept the truth of ours.

Our truth is that if we could not attend well to the minds and hearts of our children, no one in the world could. We had the luxury of beginning a new school district in a new building with a new staff. Our parents hold high expectations for their children, and our students arrive ready to learn. We took responsibility for this opportunity to rethink the purpose and delivery of secondary education.

A colleague told us recently that upon hearing that she would be teaching at our high school, her neighbor rolled his eyes and commented, sarcastically, that at least at Souhegan, her students would feel good about themselves. We cannot understand his disdain. What is wrong with creating an environment in which teenagers feel valued as long as the focus is on their academic growth and enrichment? Isn't that what we specifically seek out for our young children as they enter their first kindergarten classroom? Do our teenagers deserve less from us? Shouldn't helping adolescents to like themselves and to value their own existence be a minimal expectation of our schools? Was this man so comfortable at 14 or 16 that he can speak with derision about today's youth? We doubt it.

Our Mission Statement states that we "aspire to be a community of learners, born of respect, trust, and courage." We value an environment that asks each of us to "aspire." This word honors our intent to make a difference each day to a child. Each day, we aspire.

Our science coordinator Dan Bisaccio shakes his head when teachers dismiss his work with students as only being possible because of the context of our school. The irony is that when Dan taught in a rural school in a very poor district, people then claimed that Dan could succeed in his work because nobody really cared about that school or that town. Forming personal connections with students is not a decision limited to wealthy schools, poor schools, urban schools, or rural schools. Forming personal connections with each child should be the conscious choice of every adult charged with developing a child's mind and heart. As writer and educator Grace McEntee has said: "We cannot hope to understand all the complexities of the child standing before us. But we—all of us—with courage and intention, . . . can muster skills and mobilize grit attained through our own experience to fulfill our obligations as members of the largest village the world has ever known" (personal communication, 1999).

We are a school born of change, driven by mission, and committed to democratic practices. Our programs grew as responses to the children standing before us. In writing this text, we focused our attention on our experiences in creating standards of performance that transcend the individual classroom experiences for our students. We want to share with you our experiences in creating safe and caring structures that establish and support high expectations for each child and adult in our learning community.

WRITING THE BOOK

In the seventh year of the school, I (Peggy) applied for a sabbatical so that I could document our work. Many of us had tried to write about Souhegan for years but had found it impossible to both do the work and then write about it. We needed time and focus, and by leaving the classroom for a year, I could provide that. Bob Mackin, our founding principal, had left the school in 1998 but agreed to help capture the thoughtfulness and the chaos of creating a school. At the beginning of the writing, Bob wrote the context for the story, and both he and Jennifer Fischer-Mueller, another charter member of Souhegan's faculty, served as an editorial board for my initial draft. They posed questions, read page after page, and provided rich conversations that deepened the writing. As the work evolved, Bob took on more writing responsibility, while Jennifer continued to guide and support the work from her new post as our district's assistant superintendent.

Colleagues and students participated by sharing their work and their beliefs. As I asked them to tell me about some aspect of our school, I taped their interviews, looked for common threads, and wrote around their words. I distributed copies of all the work and revised according to feedback received. This text was truly shaped by countless conversations in hallways, lunchroom, and classrooms. Students treated me like a writer, urging me to get back to my computer whenever they saw me in the building.

At the beginning of the text, I offer the perspective of a resident of the town of Amherst, New Hampshire. I participated as a volunteer designing the educational framework of Souhegan High School and then was selected as a charter member of the Souhegan faculty. Bob Mackin narrates his experiences in moving from New York to Amherst to lead the school as our founding principal. From that point on, we both narrate the story. The reader will also "hear" many other voices in this text. If the essence of personalization is to honor individual voice, it is important to honor those voices in the writing. The reader is encouraged, therefore, to understand that the voices telling our story are the many, many past and present members of the learning community of Souhegan High School.

We have divided the text into six chapters, primarily focused around change. We begin by introducing our town and its residents and its values. We also introduce the planning team charged with establishing the structures and programs of our new school. We then write about the links between our philosophy and the programs and structures we created. We discuss the standards and practices we established for all our students and write about the progress and challenges of some of those new approaches from the perspectives of teachers and students. Maintaining these rigorous standards and the programs that support them would not be possible without a strong culture of professional development, and so we outline the supports in place for our faculty. It is important to note that we use the terms *faculty* and *teachers* in the broadest sense, to include members of our support staff and other adults who routinely interact with our students. We end this text with a study of our conscious decision to plan for change and the initiatives we are contemplating to meet the ongoing needs of our students and our community.

CHAPTER 1

The Change Process Begins

What is honored in a country is cultivated there. (Plato, *The Republic*)

Hundreds of new high schools open each year. Almost all of them continue to mirror the century-old model that seemingly served our grandparents and parents, and even some of us, reasonably well. Unfortunately, as we enter the 21st century and wrestle with the immense challenges of a new era, few of these new schools have had the courage to step out of the box and create a new model. Souhegan High School seeks to be an exception to the norm. It has consciously striven to look, to act, and to be different, all in the interest of nurturing students who are more thoughtful, more knowledgeable, and more caring. Souhegan's evolution, not simply as a new school but as a new kind of school, is chronicled in this chapter.

Here we introduce you to our community and to the beliefs that shaped our decisions. Then we begin the academic baton pass to the "planning team"—the educators who would design the initial structures and programs of Souhegan High School. We discuss their planning process in detail and outline the most consuming part of the undertaking—the hiring of an entirely new faculty. Lastly, we attempt to convey the efforts—both tangible and intangible—of the planning team to model the vision, beliefs, and values that they sought to have the entire Souhegan community embrace.

WHY A NEW HIGH SCHOOL?

Change happens slowly in our *Live Free or Die* state. A child entering kindergarten when the town of Amherst first began to study building a high school would graduate before we opened Souhegan High School in September of 1992. Our years of deliberation worked in our favor, though, as we built a much different school from the one we had first envisioned 12 years earlier.

Between 1980 and 1992, Americans experienced vast changes in almost every social institution. Acronyms entered our vocabulary. We interacted differently with our banks as we mastered ATMs; we used the health care industry differently as we confronted the intricacies of HMOs. We watched television differently as we incorporated cable and satellites and VCRs into our viewing options. In the midst of these huge societal shifts and acronym mania, however, we did not change our notion of school. Our schools remained largely unchanged from the factory model that industrialists had conceived more than a hundred years ago. Clearly, to prepare students for their future rather than our pasts, we had to prepare them for a vastly different and rapidly changing world. We had to prepare students for careers that did not yet exist, for problems that had not yet surfaced. We had to create schools that would graduate problem solvers, critical thinkers, and team players—young adults who would be smart, versatile, and caring.

The towns of Amherst and Mont Vernon had tuitioned their high school students to the neighboring town of Milford for 35 years. Each town had a different economic profile, and the mix worked well. The 1970s and early 1980s brought about a large increase in population in Amherst, Milford, and Mont Vernon, and the towns began meeting to consider options for building a new school that would accommodate the students from these three towns. Residents viewed a building program as an opportunity to acquire equal decision-making authority; the existing agreement prevented Amherst or Mont Vernon from participating in the governance of the school or holding a seat on the Milford School Board. For Dr. Richard Lalley, the superintendent of schools for Amherst and Mont Vernon, this lack of participation in the governance of the high school caused great frustration. Meetings between the school boards of the towns were mostly perfunctory in nature.

As deliberation about a new school began, residents of Amherst and Mont Vernon felt great optimism. At the same time, residents of Milford recognized that if Amherst were to pull its students out of their high school, the overcrowding issue at Milford High School would disappear for a few years; their building would still require major renovations, but at nowhere near their share of the cost of a new facility.

The three towns formed the Souhegan Valley Cooperative District in 1988. Dr. Lalley expressed his high hopes for success:

> The planning effort was exciting. We developed a $23.5 million bond issue; we found land; we developed curriculum; we marketed the whole thing. We scheduled the largest school district meeting ever held in the state and hired a sound consultant who was working on then Vice President Bush's campaign. We held the

meeting in an empty warehouse, the only place we could find for the 3,500 registered voters. We bused people in and set up an overflow room at MASH [Milford Area Senior High], with audio-visual connections. The logistics were daunting, but when the votes were counted, we fell short of the required 66²/₃% by about 300 votes.

There were so many teary-eyed people at 1:00 A.M., as the vote was announced. Such despondence; so much time had been invested by so many people. And so many kids were there; the kids felt strongly about staying together. They couldn't imagine tearing apart this student body that had been together for so many years, going back to the early 1950s. All that work, essentially for naught.

On that rainy November evening in 1988, Amherst had received its pink slip.

"Always a bridesmaid, never a bride," according to Dr. Lalley, Amherst began to seek other solutions. At times, it seemed that Amherst had invited every town east of the Mississippi to join in building a high school. Finally, in October of 1989, the citizens of Mont Vernon (population 1,800) and Amherst (population 9,000), voting separately, agreed to form a cooperative high school, alleviating some of the tax burden on the towns because cooperative districts received additional funding from the state. That vote, according to Dr. Lalley, put salve on the hurt that had formed earlier when the other co-op efforts had failed. The bridesmaid had finally become a bride.

In June of 1990, voters from the two towns overwhelmingly approved the $12.5 million bond. The new school would open with 550 students but would accommodate 800 students. The towns were confident that they had resolved issues of growth well into the second decade of the 21st century.

Years of sustained conversation about providing for our secondary school students had produced a sense of what we wanted and needed. May Balsama, long-time PTA president and chair of the first Souhegan Cooperative School Board, remembers that "people were frustrated; there was no forum in Milford for our ideas or our complaints; given that mentality, there was unrest."

Tuition without representation, a not so subtle reference to the colonial cry of taxation without representation, signaled the theme of the unrest. That unrest turned into strong community support for change; a survey of town residents provided clear direction to the planning committee. Former school board member Ann Logan believes that the constant conversation about a new school promoted the seeds of change. "Communication was the key," according to Logan. "We sponsored coffees, evening meetings in every neighborhood, on every street in town. We knew, by the time we started, what type of education residents wanted for their high school students. We also knew that the community wanted a strong voice in the planning process."

Superintendent Lalley tapped into that heightened consciousness in his call for volunteers. The 125 respondents represented a wide range of income, profession, and family demographics. Dr. Lalley provided the structure; as Ann Logan states, "he put the meat on the bones" of the conversation. He challenged the volunteers to "use their collective wisdom" to create the ideal learning environment for our students. Volunteers worked to identify building sites, to develop curriculum, to develop the technology infrastructure, to obtain financing, to design the building, to develop a sports and club program, to develop recreational facilities, and to keep the public informed. To those of us working on developing the curriculum and an initial philosophy statement, Dr. Lalley posed the following questions:

- If Souhegan High School were ideally effective for students, how would we know it? What would be happening? What would be taking place?
- In an ideal learning environment, what would students be learning, how would they learn, and how would we know that they were learning?
- In an ideal learning environment, who would teach our students, and what qualities would we want those teachers to model?
- What types of space do people need in order to produce work of the highest quality?

Focused on Dr. Lalley's challenge to change outmoded concepts of secondary schooling, the Curriculum Committee—engineers, homemakers, teachers, artists, MBAs—collectively grappled with the concept of the "ideal." Several dreamed of students who would be given time to study a topic in depth; others of a building with artists performing and artwork displayed throughout the building and the town. One committee member waxed enthusiastic about a ROTC program and hallways that were straight enough to see the entire school, so that one could, technically, fire a weapon to create order. A lead-lined gymnasium could provide space for target practice. Another individual focused on the notion of bathroom stalls comfortable enough to read his daily paper in. This heterogeneous mix of adults began to model the kinds of diverse thinking, learning styles, and abilities that the school itself would come to represent. The committee vacillated between feeling extremely capable and woefully inadequate to the task, knowing that the conceptual framework for the philosophy of teaching and learning would ultimately be used to create physical space. In retrospect, the committee realized that, in order to build a school that would mirror the values of our communities, they truly had to understand the communities and to understand their dreams for their children.

WHAT FORMS OUR SENSE OF COMMUNITY?

Incorporated in 1760, Amherst has a village center that contains a pristine town green surrounded by the Congregational Church, the Town Hall, and the Brick School, built in 1854, now the home of the office of the superintendent of schools. The library is just off the green, across the street from Carriage Road, a scenic lane of large 18th- and 19th-century "Currier and Ives" houses.

Until the 1970s, both Amherst and Mont Vernon were sleepy New England villages with stable populations; most of the towns' residents had grown up within the state's borders. The towns of Amherst and Mont Vernon today are as adolescent as their teenagers. A population surge more than doubled the number of residents between 1970 and 1990, as the technology belt around Boston imported managers from around the country. By 1999, Souhegan High School's eighth year, the town of Amherst had 12,000 residents. Demographically, the town had evolved from a rural, colonial village to a medium-sized bedroom community. One native of the town reported that she had to join a newcomers' group to become acquainted with the people who now lived in her hometown.

Located only an hour's drive from Boston, the mountains, and the seacoast, Amherst and Mont Vernon have retained their colonial charm. Primarily college-educated, upper-middle-class communities, both towns enjoy a reputation for historic preservation, diligent planning, and a commitment to education. The vast majority of residents of the state, as well as the towns of Amherst and Mont Vernon, are Caucasian; the most recent census lists fewer than 125 minority residents for both towns.

Town Meetings provided the financial decision making for the towns until 1998. Residents gathered every March, agreeing to tax themselves for the coming year based on the community's town and school needs. A local service organization sponsored lunch for the Saturday meetings until someone pointed out that it was remarkably uncharitable to serve beans to people forced to spend several hours together following this meal. Girl Scouts lined the halls to sell their cookies, the PTA sold tickets to its annual musical, and neighbors wandered about greeting old friends. Everybody brought their newspapers and their knitting, prepared to sit for hours.

The merits of each warrant article were argued with great passion, and, usually, good humor. New England town meetings evoke a Norman Rockwell setting, and both towns had their unique cast of characters: the avuncular town moderator with his handlebar mustache and twinkling eyes; the resident who always informed the assembly of his reasons for every single vote he would eventually cast; the mellifluous participant who monitored our adherence to *Robert's Rules of Order*; the ardent conservationist who advocated fiercely for wetlands and open space; the fiscal conservative who once arrived dressed as Santa Claus because, in his view, we usually gave presents to anyone who asked for money. Recreation advocates would arrive en masse to speak to the need for more sports' fields, and the volunteer Rescue Squad and volunteer Fire Department would give us the repair bills for their aging equipment; sometimes, their presentation would be interrupted by the need to respond to an emergency. The rule of thumb at this annual event was that the smaller the amount requested, the longer the debate. The multimillion-dollar town or school budget was usually passed by the hundred or so residents who could stay out past 11:00 at night. On exceptionally cold evenings, friends on opposite sides of a key issue would call each other, urging each other to stay home by the warm fire. After all, if both attended Town Meeting they would simply cancel out each other's vote. This good-natured bickering produced active citizens. Changing demographics brought an end to this tradition in Amherst in 1998, although Mont Vernon still retains its town meeting.

Politically, Amherst and Mont Vernon are conservative towns in a conservative state. Candidates for statewide office proudly take the pledge to vote against state income taxes or sales taxes. New Hampshire relies on property taxes and lotteries to support its schools. Republican presidential candidates tour the town of Amherst routinely, guaranteed a base of strong support. Once every 4 years, the annual Fourth of July parade is usurped by presidential candidates hoping to gain voter recognition before the nation's first primary vote in the February of each election year. In contrast, the town's entire Democratic contingent can almost be contained on their float. Although partisan politics does not affect the governance of the town, the conservative flavor of its residents guarantees that discussion will take years before any expenditures are approved.

Family life governs the free time of Amherst and Mont Vernon residents; most children are involved in sports and recreational activities sponsored by town and school. Resident May Balsama believes that a spirit of volunteerism characterized the town when she moved there from Massachusetts in the early 1970s.

Every town has a character to it, and when you move in, you become an essential part of that character. We knew that moving to Amherst meant that we would participate, *be required to participate*, come hell or high water, and so we searched for our niche. Everybody in town belonged to the Newcomers' Club for years and years and years. You committed to your niche, whether it was the church, the Rescue Squad, the Friends of the library, the volunteer Fire Department, a service club, or the schools. Membership connected us to this community. My first volunteer job was as a head-lice checker at the elementary school, and I still have friends today that I met during that unique activity! But we all belonged to something that benefited the town or the schools.

WHAT WERE OUR BELIEFS AS WE BEGAN TO BUILD OUR SCHOOL?

To equip the volunteers with the background they needed to construct a philosophy for Souhegan High School, Dr. Lalley presented a reading list to orient them to current research on teaching and learning.

We didn't want to create a carbon copy of failure. We wanted every kid to count, to have equal weight in our hearts and in our classrooms; everyone would need to be included. What we found in our research was that we did not have to begin this reform effort alone. We found, in *Horace's Compromise* (1984), and later in *Horace's School* (1992), Dr. Ted Sizer's work, a nationwide reform effort, the Coalition of Essential Schools, that we could tie ourselves to, that we could work with other like-minded people who wanted to make high schools better.

The final plan presented by the Curriculum Committee and accepted by the Souhegan School Board included an organizational structure with a principal, an assistant principal, two division heads, one for arts and humanities and another for math, science, and technology. Teachers would serve on academic teams, replacing a traditional departmental structure. Schedules would allow for longer periods of learning.

Beginning the search for the principal challenged the committee. In brainstorming for qualities of effective leadership, we noted that we wanted the successful candidate to have the ability to walk on water and see the future clearly.

The Search Committee was adamant that the position of principal be designed as one with primary time and resources committed to academic rather than managerial concerns. They firmly believed that corollary tasks of the administrative team would clearly be secondary to the demands of academic leadership.

The Souhegan School Board and the Principal Search Committee then placed an advertisement for the principal in several national publications, receiving 55 responses from 24 states and 3 countries. We interviewed 12 candidates for the position. What we needed was a visionary with managerial experience who saw the potential in creating the ideal learning environment. While the search team initially held different perspectives about hiring someone from out of state, the final vote for Dr. Robert Mackin, a New York educator, was unanimous.

In the following section, Bob offers his perspective of the challenges of building a new school and hiring a new staff.

Robert Mackin, Founding Principal

Like many principals, I always try to stay abreast of the educational job market even when I have no desire to change jobs at the time. For many of us the Sunday *New York Times* has become a key employment "database." Thus, it was on a Sunday in the spring of 1991, while I was leisurely perusing the *Times*, that an advertisement for the principalship of a yet-to-be-built high school in New Hampshire caught my eye.

At the time, I was employed, on most days quite happily, as principal of a well-respected public high school in suburban Westchester County, New York, about 45 minutes north of New York City. My leadership had come to be highly regarded by the community, so I had no anxieties about having to leave. Moreover, I had the security of an excellent retirement system and was one of the highest-paid principals in the country. Looking for a new job was not within the realm of my thinking. Nevertheless, there was something enticing about this particular ad:

> NEW PRINCIPAL NEEDED
> NEW HIGH SCHOOL DISTRICT
> NEW HIGH SCHOOL
> NEW STAFF
> NEW BEGINNING

The Souhegan Cooperative School Board is seeking an experienced educational leader to be Principal of its high school which opens in September, 1992.

Employment will begin on or about July 8, 1991, a year in advance of
school opening, to allow time to hire faculty and develop curriculum.

An outstanding opportunity for an innovative educator.

The dream of most of us high school principals is to someday have
the chance to start our own school, to hire a faculty from scratch, to design
the perfect environment for kids and teachers. For those of us committed
to living in the Northeast, this dream rarely comes to fruition. Old school
designs, veteran teachers, and worn-out facilities seem to be the norm here.
Over the past 10 years, perhaps a dozen new high schools have been opened
in New England. Even some of those have merely been new facilities in
communities where union or other contractual agreements have required
the hiring of existing district teachers. Suffice it to say, being able to implement the new school dream is a rarity. Consequently, as I read this ad, it
resonated for me in a very different way.

When I arrived at the last few lines, however, my initial enthusiasm
quickly faded. As an 11-year resident of the relatively liberal state of New
York, and having worked over this period of time with a mostly progressive group of teachers, I was chagrined to find that the location of this
school-to-be was in some small town in New Hampshire.

As a New Yorker, my first impressions of New Hampshire were "Live
Free or Die" license plates, John Sununu as governor and subsequent adviser
to Ronald Reagan, and the *Manchester Union Leader* newspaper. While the
intense Yankee independence proclaimed on the auto tags didn't deter me,
the idea of a truly "new school for the 21st century" arising in the conservative climate of Sununu politics and William Loeb's right-wing diatribes in the
state's largest newspaper was in fact troubling. How could the school envisioned in this ad truly take root in such a politically barren wilderness?

It was time, nevertheless, to do a bit of intensive soul searching. As I
reflected on my professional aspirations, I was deeply struck for the first
time by the slow pace of change and by the abrasive voices of the nay-say-
ers in most high schools. New Hampshire began to take on more appeal
and was worth at least an exploratory look.

My letter of interest to the superintendent included a sense of who I
was and what I had accomplished professionally, but more than that it listed
a set of dreams and aspirations about what schools might truly become. It
was a letter that also expressed frank skepticism about the willingness of
this particular school district to commit itself to the very general vision of
a school as described in this small ad in the *New York Times*.

Thereafter the process took on a momentum of its own. Through a
mutual feeling-out process, the Principal Search Committee and I inter-

viewed each other. They wanted to figure out whether I was as good as I made myself sound and whether I really was lunatic enough to take a $35,000 pay cut in order to have the chance to start a new school. I wanted to know if they were prepared to deal with the political rejection that they would inevitably experience in a smart, upper-middle-class community where their own innovative thinking would likely conflict with the mainstream view, namely that good schooling should look like a remake of a private academy.

If I were to become its founding leader, this new school would certainly not be like an exclusive New England prep school or even like a typical wealthy suburban high school. While these places are wonderful educational institutions where elite clienteles are provided with enriched opportunities, they also represent a very limited conception of instructional practice. Certainly "our" new school would aspire to the same high academic standards, but our means of challenging kids to reach those expectations would be far different—far more engaging, student-centered, and performance-driven. Therefore, I needed to know if they could support the kinds of programs that we would seek to undertake.

To the credit of the school board and the superintendent, the commitment to creating a true "school for the 21st century" was a real one. My primary concerns were allayed. They were indeed seeking a principal who could pursue a dramatically new vision formulated around the kinds of principles expressed by the Coalition of Essential Schools. Over the next month, I finally convinced my wife, a born-and-bred New Yorker, that this change would be good for us. At the end of June 1991, I took the job.

While the transition to New Hampshire culture was not always an easy one for our family, the professional opportunity afforded was truly unique. Here was the chance to put into place all the rhetoric that I had become so fond of espousing.

My first task, and perhaps the most critical one in the entire undertaking, involved the hiring of a leadership team who would work with me during our initial year of planning and design. Fortunately the new Souhegan Cooperative School Board had the foresight to recognize that the opening of a brand-new high school could not be a one-person show that would debut overnight. A year of planning had been prescribed before the projected school opening in September 1992. Moreover, the board had budgeted for five positions to support in the design and implementation:

Director of guidance
Head librarian
Division coordinator of math, science, and technology
Division coordinator of humanities
Principal's secretary

Fortunately, I had served previously as an administrator in five different settings—a K–12 alternative school director; a university-based project director; a suburban high school director of curriculum and instruction; a suburban middle school principal; and, most recently, principal of the high school on the same campus. Consequently, I was quite aware of my own leadership strengths, propensities, inadequacies, and idiosyncrasies; and I knew what type of support would be most beneficial both to me and to the school.

I needed people who had similar philosophical beliefs about teaching and learning and cared about kids in the same ways that I did. But I also needed people who were highly task-focused and capable of putting into place the often idealistic notions that I brought to the table. I wanted a balance of idealism and wisdom, of experience tempered with fresh thinking, of perfectionism mixed with heavy doses of realism, and of people who truly believed that all young people could be challenged to meet high standards. There was no doubt in my mind that this first round of hiring would set a tone, establish an expectation of excellence, and create a symbol of what a truly collaborative team could be.

My first call was to an old friend of 20 years and a former colleague on two previous occasions, Cleve Penberthy. Cleve had recently stepped down as superintendent of schools of Telluride, Colorado, where he had first served as principal in 1980. I knew that he was restless and looking for a new challenge and that, more importantly, he was one of the best educators with whom I had ever worked. He was outstanding with kids, shared my educational views wholeheartedly, and was bright, charismatic, articulate, and unflappable. He also had an old New Hampshire connection that later proved to be helpful—he was a 1970 graduate of Dartmouth College.

Cleve had also grown up in the same hometown as I did—Norwalk, Connecticut—and was a public school guy like me. Because of his administrative experience, I wanted Cleve to take on more than a director of guidance role. At the same time, I wanted to create a different conception of student services/guidance that blended the role of counselor, disciplinarian, and student advocate in a way that was not unlike the role a good parent would play. I viewed Cleve as the ideal model to accomplish this new approach as our first dean of students.

Simultaneous with Cleve's hiring, I sifted through résumés for the two academic coordinator positions. I found the narrowing of choices to be relatively easy in the humanities. The ultimate choice, Allison Rowe, was a perfect match both for me and for the school. In her application, mailed just hours before the deadline, Allison indicated that she had just drawn her line in the sand. "Caught up," she stated, "in an upheaval due to inept and inappropriate administrative actions that turned teachers and administrators into combatants," she was ready for a change. Her academic credentials included degrees from Smith College and Dartmouth, but she credited her belief in education reform to her experience watching her mother's work as a teacher in a rural one-room schoolhouse. There she observed "older students teaching younger, a diversified curriculum that offered something in the same unit to the 6-year-old and the 12-year-old . . . cooperative learning groups, . . . experiential education at the core of all the learning." In her mother's school, "if the older boys had failed to split the day's supply of firewood, the children would have been unable to learn. And learning was at the core—getting an education was a way out of the hard-scrabble farming most of the children faced daily." These core beliefs and experiences shaped Allison's work at Souhegan High School for the next 7 years.

From a political perspective, Allison's New Hampshire roots helped to defuse the image that good educational leaders had to be carpetbaggers imported from places like New York or Colorado.

For me personally, Allison represented the highly task-focused, nononsense approach that I needed to temper my own propensity to philosophize and play with big ideas. While Allison could hold her own intellectually with anyone, she also had a low level of tolerance for extended discussions. Consequently, one of her great contributions to the planning team later on was to keep us grounded, to hold us quickly to task when conversations drifted or became long-winded.

Locating her a math/science/technology compatriot was much more difficult. Ideally, I hoped to find an outstanding science teacher/leader who also had a strong math background. The likelihood of finding the opposite experience base—a mathematician with strong science skills—would be pretty slim from what I had seen in my own experiences as a high school administrator. Therefore, I recruited from a list of the past 10 years' Presidential Award winners. My hope was to find a person who could lead and clearly articulate a vision of science teaching that incorporated the best thinking of the National Science Teachers Association [NSTA], of the 2061 Project, and so forth. Likewise, this individual should be able to build a math curriculum modeled on the National Council of Teachers of Mathematics [NCTM] standards, an integrated approach that blended mathematical concepts.

I sent more than 100 letters to this prospective group of applicants. To my surprise and delight, six of these Presidential Award winners applied and all were interviewed. Very quickly, Dan Bisaccio rose to the top as our choice, a man Ted Sizer characterized as the best "Essential School" teacher he had ever observed. Ironically, when my letter arrived at Dan's house, his wife opened it and called to inform me that Dan was the right person for the job but was currently in the Soviet Union, serving as part of an American delegation of educators. Dan proved to be worth the wait, and we offered him the job on the spot.

As he looked at the clutter of our workspace, Dan was fond of quoting a farmer who had once told him that "a clean stall means a dead horse." He wanted "to find teachers with good instincts, people who knew their subjects well enough to be playful with it, instead of those who liked to impose their knowledge on others, in particular, children."

The last professional staff member to join our planning team was information specialist Kim Carter, former New Hampshire Teacher-of-the-Year and a middle school librarian. Kim had become a nationally recognized leader and proponent for the concept of libraries as information centers. Her strong background and interest in using technology as part of the design focus of information services in our new school was the final selling point in her selection.

One other position was also filled early upon my arrival in Amherst. I wanted an administrative assistant who would do most of the nitty-gritty work that I disliked doing. Nancy Baker, a secretary in one of the local elementary schools, was excited about the possibilities I outlined and eager to take on a broader leadership role. With a BA degree in classics and an MA in Egyptology, Nancy represented a symbol of our break-the-mold view. True to her aspirations, she soon changed jobs at Souhegan as she pursued her love of classical languages by teaching Latin, one of our most popular courses.

The planning team began their work in August of 1991. From that moment, the school that would open to the communities of Amherst and Mont Vernon would rely on the experiences and beliefs of these individuals. Cleve Penberthy describes his experiences during that planning year.

Cleve Penberthy, Dean of Students

In the early summer of 1991, in the box canyon ski town of Telluride, Colorado, I had just completed my 20th year of working with kids in America's schools. I had started on my hands and knees with little kids in a church basement in Harlem in 1970 and then, two decades later, found myself looking at schooling from the perspective of the superintendency at 9,000 feet in the Rocky Mountains. Professionally that spring, after graduating another class of seniors, I began to feel the onset of the "itch"—the restlessness that was nudging me to begin to think about striking out again in search of a new educational challenge. And then, as if he had been eavesdropping on my mental meanderings, Bob called from New Hampshire.

We had been around the educational block with each other twice before in our careers—once in the early 1970s at the University of Massachusetts and the National Alternative Schools Program, and later as administrators at Staples High School in Westport, Connecticut. We knew each other well. Like a tournament-tough doubles team, we anticipated each other's moves, respected each other's gifts, and had a true and unconditional sense of confidence in each other. We came to know, through the grist of living through important decisions together in the 1970s, how we each responded to pressure, to politics, to parents, to the press, to the police, and probably to the president, if he had happened to call. So when Bob laid out, long distance, his decision, he grabbed my attention again. Something big was going to be happening in Amherst.

When my wife and I made the geographic and existential leap to leave the East in 1980 to start a family and for me to assume my first principalship in Telluride, we vowed not to look back, but to keep growing a future in the West. Life was good beyond the reach of the *New York Times* and the breathtaking pace of the Washington–Boston corridor. Now the question was whether the creative career possibilities at Souhegan would or should outweigh the lifestyle we had established in Colorado. The decision was not an easy one. Finally, I gave up all rational analysis and took Yogi Berra's advice: "When you come to a fork in the road, take it." I loaded the U-Haul with my 8-year-old daughter, Eli, riding shotgun and pointed east in the direction of Kansas.

There was no question in my mind, heading east, that Bob understood how vitally important it was to assemble a high-powered, imaginative, yet grounded team of in-the-trench practitioners.

I had a fancy title, dean of students, but no kids during the planning year. Our future students were trying to focus on their last year at Milford Area Senior High (MASH), while their hometowns were buzzing about all the great things Souhegan was hoping to provide them the following year. My "students" weren't too convinced. In fact, I was greeted with a good deal of overt resistance and hostility from the kids as I gently tried to enter their culture in Milford. I needed kids involved with me from the beginning. I wanted them to know I respected what they were currently being asked to do in the name of schooling at MASH, but I needed their time to think bigger thoughts. Brian Irwin and Bill Dod, two key and respected assistant principals at MASH, helped me navigate through the halls at MASH. I needed their trust as I sought ways to engage the future Souhegan student body.

I met with voluntary groups of kids throughout the fall of 1991, beginning to plant the seeds of students' rights and responsibilities; to listen to their hopes, to comfort their fears, to talk about bells and lockers and smoking and parking spaces and team colors and mascots and cafeteria food and student government and dances—the stuff that matters and defines high school for teenagers in Amherst, Mont Vernon, and everywhere else I had helped to run schools in the past. The content of my conversations with the MASH kids was never as important as the way I wanted them to feel treated by me. They needed to know that the adults at Souhegan were going to be genuinely committed to listening to who they were, to what they hoped for, to how they wanted to grow their school. I was on point, walking gently into the habits, patterns, and history of who they were as a group of really good kids.

Students in many schools today have no reason to believe that what they say will make much of a difference in the life and flavor of their school. Plan Spirit Week? Yes. Figure out where to put the Coke machine? Yes. But how they might split the atom of learning apart, unleashing new energies and possibilities into their future? No way. While teaching and learning were front and center for much of our early planning team conversations, I kept calling on the team to puzzle over how we were going to consciously construct a different kind of culture and community the following year—a place where kids would act and react and choose ways of deciding and behaving that were guided by the values of respect, civility, and decency. Could we build an ethos that would govern our relationships with each other born of tolerance and empathy, not adversarial rules and prohibitions? Could we imagine and sustain a democracy that challenged and cared for the best in each other? Could Souhegan be a place where all of its members get better at being smart and good, while being appreciative of the complexity and beauty of life?

Occasionally, the air would be let out of our lofty intentions. "Hey, what I really want to know is what's going to happen if I cut class at your dumb school? Are you going to let us leave at lunch? Will the seniors have special privileges? How am I going to get into college if you don't have a rank-in-class, or weight classes or separate the smart kids from the dumb ones?"

Bob intuited the magic of our team when he hired us. While we had our moments, we never lost sight of the value and importance of taking care of each other through our disagreements. We kept our eyes on the target of building an important school where no school had existed before. Acting, rather than being acted upon, has always been my simple definition of creativity. Never before, and possibly never again, will I feel the personal and professional exhilaration of making something great happen from nothing like we did in giving birth to Souhegan High School during our 1991–1992 planning year.

"MAKING THE IDEAL REAL"

The office that would serve as the high school for the planning year had been the town's first high school. Known as the Brick School, our office, a large room lined with chalkboards, spanned the width of the building. Large windows filled with light faced the town green and the Congregational Church. Downstairs, Jack and Jill Kindergarten filled the air with young voices. According to Kim Carter,

> In every conversation around that big conference table in that drafty room, everything was up for grabs. The ultimate questions were "Why?" and "How does this impact student learning?" Every decision was preceded by the question of what difference it would make in the life of a child. Consequently, we questioned all our assumptions, even things a school normally takes for granted, like the bus schedule. Every meeting had a true "think tank" quality in that every suggestion went through the filters of impact on student learning. The room afforded little privacy, so we all overheard Cleve grilling the candidates for guidance counselor positions. "So, okay, some girl tells you she's pregnant. How do you handle *that*? . . . Suppose you find out he's smoking dope? Do you call his parents?" . . . etc. as if these things were immediate crises that this candidate had to handle before getting out of the interview.

What made that planning year work, according to Nancy Baker, was that:

> The team modeled in each other what we meant to offer our students— a tiny community of trust and respect and courage working with the passion, heart, and commitment that we brought with us and forged together. Nothing shaped us more than that first year of making the ideal real.

CHAPTER 2

From Mindset to Mission

An organization Mission Statement—one that truly reflects the deep, shared vision and values of everyone within that organization— creates a great unity and tremendous commitment. It creates in people's hearts and minds a frame of reference, a set of criteria or guidelines, by which they will govern themselves. They don't need someone else directing, controlling, criticizing, or taking cheap shots. They have brought the changeless core of what the organization is about. (Covey, 1990, p. 143)

While the community task force had created an image of a new high school and presented a wide array of ideas, it was now up to the planning team to bring tangible shape to it. In this chapter, we attempt to capture the essence and flavor of the planning year, August 1991–August 1992. After quickly outlining the key ingredients of Souhegan—the practices, structures, and key design elements that would embody the school—attention focused on writing a formal mission statement. Similar to the heads of most corporate cultures, the leaders of Souhegan believed that a clear sense of mission would bring both consistency and coherence to its culture. As related in this chapter, what they found was surprising. Unlike most high schools, the role of the Souhegan "mission" takes on an almost supernatural importance, as it drives every action of the school.

Establishing clear communications with the community emerges as an important next step. And then, as the year unfolds, the planning team finds itself being carried along by a natural momentum as the hiring process takes on a life of its own and dominates the second half of the planning year. The chapter closes with some vignettes from the first gathering of the new Souhegan faculty—3 weeks of planning and orientation in August 1992—and addresses some key issues that surfaced to bring shape to a new and emerging professional culture.

THE PLANNING TEAM

From the outset, every aspect of planning needed to be examined within a holistic context, for any single decision would affect the next decision. All the components would need to fit and make sense in order for the school as a whole to work. In practical terms, this meant that the mission of the school had to drive the design of curriculum, which would lead to decisions about instruction, assessment, relationships with students, and school policies.

The planning team, in an early October 1991 meeting, agreed within an hour's time that the following "givens" would frame the new school design and implementation:

- A clearly articulated mission to drive the actions of the school
- Heterogeneous grouping and inclusion of all students
- Core curriculum with "less is more" philosophy
- Curriculum based on essential questions
- Teachers acting as coach/facilitators
- Advisory groups at all grade levels
- Emphasis on interdisciplinary curriculum
- Honors challenges available to all interested students in all classes
- Teams of English, math, science, and social studies teachers at grades 9 and 10
- Interdisciplinary teams of teachers, if possible, at other grade levels, including a mandatory senior seminar
- All teams having common blocks of teaching time and of planning time
- All classes meeting for at least one extended time block during the week
- An integrated math program in grades 9–11
- An integrated science program in grades 9–10 at least
- An adventure-based physical education program
- An integrated arts program
- Technology integrated into core curriculum, not separate classes
- Foreign language built on a communicative approach
- Performance assessment (with clearly defined rubrics) and portfolios expected of all students
- Senior Project as a final culminating exhibition for all graduating students
- Professional development built on teacher collaborative work
- Democratic decision making, including a Community Council with student voice

- Grading based on A, B, C system; anything less than a C- not to receive credit (NC)
- No departmental structure

Once these basic principles had been established, three agenda items were immediately placed on the docket:

1. Writing the Mission Statement
2. Creating communication channels with the community
3. Hiring a staff

THE MISSION STATEMENT

The creation of the Mission Statement itself, which to this day has remained an unchanged and essential force in shaping and directing Souhegan High School, took several days of intensive debate and conversation on the part of the planning team.

Beginning with the philosophical outline provided by the volunteer Curriculum Committee and with the "givens" noted above, the team decided that to be easily read and understood, the mission statement should be succinct, powerful, and written in the form of a bullet list. It needed to be short enough to be displayed on walls and catch a reader's attention, provocative enough to engender interest and raise expectations, and inclusive enough to capture the essence of what this new school aspired to be. After many hours of discussion, the planning team wrote the final version of the Mission Statement:

Souhegan High School aspires to be a community of learners born of respect, trust, and courage. We consciously commit ourselves:
>   To support and engage an individual's unique gifts, passions, and intentions.
>   To develop and empower the mind, body, and heart.
>   To challenge and expand the comfortable limits of thought, tolerance, and performance.
>   To inspire and honor the active stewardship of family, nation, and globe.

The importance of rhythm and flow were also taken into account; for example, each of the bulleted sections begins with an infinitive and is then followed by two verbs and three nouns. Word choices took hours of deliberation. The deliberate inclusion of the word *passion* caused great angst initially, but we did not want to compromise the intent behind the word choice. Who could argue with the lofty ideal expressed by the word *passion* in an educational environment?

The Souhegan School Board agreed that the Mission Statement reflected the beliefs and values they held for the school. Henceforth, it became the school's founding document, emblazoned in bold calligraphy in the front lobby.

Embedded in the document is the set of beliefs that our school is a humane, caring, and personalized school—a school where all students are welcome, are known well, and are heard, and therefore a place where all students feel a stake in the institution, not simply in their own success.

Consequently, the mission became central to fostering essential academic goals. Students learn to think best, to use their minds well, to try out ideas, to express their views, to interact in teams, and to absorb themselves in a dynamic learning process in an environment where they feel trusted, respected, and encouraged. Building from the mission, we engendered a mindset in the faculty that *all* students unequivocally and without question can and will learn and that teachers must actively engage *all* students in meaningful and nonthreatening ways.

It is worth thinking about this concept of mission for a moment. Historically, most institutions, including schools, have a statement of philosophy or mission—a public commitment to a set of beliefs or values that drive the institution. Unfortunately, in practical terms, these statements often have little significance. In the case of schools they appear in glossy documents—the front of the Program of Studies or perhaps in the appendix to the annual report to the board of education. Every 10 years they are pulled from shelves and dusted off for the regional accreditation visit. Rarely does a Mission Statement serve as a true basis for designing school programs or affecting teacher practice.

In Souhegan's case, a very different phenomenon occurs. The Mission Statement acts as a daily guide for action and is the basis for defining very human expectations. The Mission Statement is such a powerful force in the school culture that students at times feel annoyed by continually having it in their face.

Unlike an alternative school of 80 to 100 students where the emphasis upon personalization and individual stakeholding is relatively easy to achieve, in a school of 900 students and 100 adults, implementation of these values becomes more difficult. A conscious and consistent focus on mission is essential if those values are to become embraced by the entire school community.

For Souhegan High School, the Mission Statement provides the "curriculum" for the first part of each schoolyear. On the opening day of school, Advisory groups of ten students and one adult meet for the first hour or so and focus on the new school year—both the pragmatic and the philosophical. The Mission Statement is the centerpiece for these conversations, and Advisory groups serve as the backbone of the school culture. Words like *respect* and *trust*—the values that are most embedded in the culture—are defined, redefined, and absorbed through tangible examples.

Advisory groups, which meet daily over the course of the year, talk about issues such as responsibility and freedom within the context of civil and respectful interpersonal conversations. We developed a handbook for all advisers to help to ensure that some consistency of focus occurred by grade level. Ultimately, the adviser becomes the adult who knows his students as well as a surrogate parent.

While some students find the constant concern about mission to be a bit obsessive, the need for ongoing reinforcement of beliefs and values is essential to the maintenance of a healthy and lasting school culture. For the ninth-graders, the focus is most intense. The team-taught freshman humanities curriculum has as its essential question, "What does it mean to be an American?" As prelude to a study of the nation's founding documents, the Declaration of Independence and the United States Constitution, ninth-graders examine and discuss the Mission Statement as the founding document of Souhegan High School (SHS). Consequently, words such as *respect* and *trust* take on real meaning and gradually the overall programs and structure of SHS, which seemed very different and even confusing, begin to make more sense to them. In turn, the concept of culture is addressed. American democratic culture is dissected by looking at the attributes that had led to our country's success in fostering democratic values over a 200-year period. Then Souhegan High School is defined as their own home base for democratic practice, a place where they have a voice and ongoing opportunities to engage in true democratic decision making.

It is easy to articulate the reasons for student ownership of the concepts stated in the Mission Statement, but for it to be a dynamic life force in the school community, its tenets must resonate for all members. We ask students to draw connections between their work and the Mission Statement in reflections at the end of units of study, in their community service work, in their Advisories, and more formally during their Senior Project and their Division One Exhibition. Adult connections to the Mission Statement tend to be more implicit than explicit.

Language coordinator Marcia Arndt reflects on the first time she saw the Mission Statement as she waited in the main hallway for her job interview:

I stood contemplating it for the longest time. It was the first time I would work in a school with an articulated and public Mission Statement. The goals and ideals seemed to be written expressly for me, to let me know that this educational environment would be dependent on a strong sense of community learning. It felt so right and so comfortable to me as I stood there.

The ensuing years have shown me the tension that indeed exists between the ideal and the real. However, the very fact that we have a stated sense of who we are and that we have an ideal to consistently attempt to reach makes a difference to me. The line between expert and novice blurs in an atmosphere of continual learning.

When Steve Dreher became the faculty adviser to the school newspaper, *The Saber Scribe*, he was determined to teach his staff to "push the comfortable limits of thought, tolerance, and performance." Steve says:

In my family, we revel in dissent. We are a large family, and our arguments often serve as means of communication, but we always enjoy these encounters, the expression of different perspectives. We always join forces in the end, despite our individual beliefs. That's what communities do; that is what I want my writers and editors to do—to measure the daily school culture against the ideal, and to call the gaps to everyone's attention. That is also what I want to begin to do myself in a more public fashion—to push my colleagues' comfortable limits and to invite them to push mine. That kind of energy will sustain our personal and professional growth.

Conservation biology teacher Melissa Chapman finds the blueprint for her work in Souhegan's Mission Statement:

Both my students and I are encouraged to pursue our gifts, passions, and intentions. Collaboration with the scientific community gives my students authentic contexts for their learning and contributes to a mutual understanding of human impact on global systems. By doing the work of scientists, my students become active stewards of their environment.

ACTION STEPS AND TIMELINE

Our earliest planning days were consumed by program issues and practical concerns within the school, from the most philosophical—de-

veloping a position paper on heterogeneous groupings and honors challenges—to the most practical—ordering tables and chairs; from the most
student-centered—meeting with students about the transition from Milford
Area Senior High School to Souhegan High School—to the most teacher-
focused—creating a list of personnel benefits. Other than in smaller alternative or charter schools, few precedents existed elsewhere for developing a high school that would be so different in so many ways.

We were helped by the variety of visitors who saw a unique opportunity to share in and perhaps influence the direction of a school that promised to become a state model and a national focal point for rethinking secondary education. The Brick School became a bastion of school reform.

The vast majority of the public were not fully aware of the progressive deliberations that had established Souhegan's foundation. From a very
practical standpoint, most citizens were more interested in having a high
school as a community focal point for the first time, with athletic teams,
concerts, dramatic events, scholarship nights, and the like—all those trappings of high school that they had experienced themselves. Few people
were initially aware of the unique nature of the new school or of the pre-
dispositions of the school board or of the new administrative team.

With this as a backdrop, I (Bob) took the lead in a major outreach effort that was initiated to inform the two communities of the programs that
were being proposed and the rationale for the many new initiatives. Having experienced community backlash to concepts such as heterogeneous
grouping in my previous principalship, I pushed the team to be visible and
proactive in its communication with the public.

The first major step was a community newsletter sent to all local house-
holds in November 1991 that provided an update of all the work done thus
far in the planning process. More importantly, it outlined the key principles
that would serve as the underpinnings of the school—from mixed ability
groups to senior exhibitions, from a focus on depth of understanding to
the role of teachers as coaches, from Advisory groups to teacher teaming
and interdisciplinary curriculum.

The newsletter, in turn, led to a series of community meetings where
any resident of the two towns could meet the new administrative team,
hear about proposed programs, provide their input, and ask questions.
Lively and provocative discussions quickly became the norm. While most
of the conversations were courteous and positive in tone, heated debates
began to arise within a small segment of the public around the issues of
interdisciplinary instruction and mixed ability grouping, particularly the
idea that the school would not have honors classes per se. This debate
would later spill over into a school district referendum vote on the basic
philosophy of the school in March 1993.

In the meantime, community meetings, regular newsletters, speeches to the local service clubs, a series of supportive news stories, and the unintended payoffs of meeting with our students-to-be on a regular basis reaped major dividends. The concept of a very new and different high school came to be viewed in a largely positive light. Likewise, as the planning year proceeded, a high degree of optimism pervaded the community's thinking. This growing enthusiasm for the school, fostered by the strong public relations efforts noted above, set the tone for the opening year and clearly helped the school weather its first major test—the referendum vote held in March 1993. By an 8–1 margin, the 500 community members present at the school district meeting voted overwhelmingly in support of the major premises of the school: heterogeneous grouping and interdisciplinary teaching.

In spite of the frenetic nature of work in the Brick School, our office in the historic center of Amherst, the energy was clearly focused on the big picture, on creating a school that would make a difference in the lives of kids, staff, and the community.

Our students-to-be, as a first step in recognizing the value we would place on listening to their voices, were charged with choosing a school mascot. The ultimate vote went to the saber-toothed tiger, which nosed out the aardvark, the weasel, and other clever suggestions. While some of us questioned the symbolism of choosing an extinct mammal as the mascot, the importance of listening to students was established at the outset, and so we became the "Sabers." Future Souhegan student Tilea Warren then designed a wonderful saber-toothed tiger logo that has subsequently served for the duration of the school's existence.

THE HIRING PROCESS

The magnitude of hiring 55 professionals promised to be staggering, particularly given the word-of-mouth publicity we had already received and the resulting flood of informal applicants. We decided to place formal advertisements in December.

Perhaps our most careful thinking as a team went into the design of our application process. We wanted to first meet prospective teachers as reflective practitioners. To that end, we asked candidates to write a detailed letter/essay in response to the following prompts:

- What have you done to raise the academic achievement of all high school students, including the at-risk and the gifted?
- Given the "vision" of Souhegan High School reflected in the enclosed newsletter, how might you structure your ideal position at

the school so that you could be an effective teacher and member of the school community?

- What adjectives would students and colleagues use to describe you in your present work setting?
- Discuss a significant educational issue you have addressed in your classroom or larger school community and strategies you initiated to solve it.
- How have new technologies affected your teaching and student learning?
- Discuss any significant experiences you have had as an athletic coach, mentor, club or class adviser, and current coaching interests.
- Discuss a quotation, piece of literature, person whom you respect, or experience that has impacted on your work or life.
- What do you do for fun?

We wanted a clear image of how they wrote, how they thought, how they would persist through a much more arduous process than most teaching applications required. Of the initial 1,300 inquiries for packets, 700 completed applications were submitted and several hundred interviews were held.

While most of the applications resulted from newspaper advertising, many of our strongest candidates came via friends calling friends and spreading the word about this progressive new school soon to be emerging in New Hampshire. Applications arrived from as far away as Montana, Colorado, and Chicago. Without consciously trying, we had extended our search beyond the bounds of New York and New England. The applicant pool, to our surprise and subsequent good fortune, had become national in scope.

For those of us on the planning team, the reading of applications and the resulting interview process was the most intense experience of our lives. Beginning in mid-February, we broke into interview teams with at least two of us sitting in on each of the interviews. Most interviews lasted close to an hour. Given the extensive work we had expected candidates to have completed during the application process, it seemed only fair to grant them sufficient time to present themselves in person.

An easy rhythm soon developed, and each of our unique interview styles emerged. Cleve was quick to jump into scenarios: "Suppose a kid reeks of marijuana when he comes into your class? What are you going to say to him?" Kim pushed and prodded people on their use of technology and their willingness to be learners themselves. Allison and Dan probed hard on classroom expertise and the depth of a teacher's knowledge base beyond his or her own subject area. I usually asked them to "tell us what your students would say about you if we had a dozen of them in a room? What kinds of adjectives would they use to describe you?" Most candidates were highly energized by the process.

We had a chance to interact with some extraordinary people, many of whom were hired on the spot. Among our resulting crew was a lawyer, a minister-in-training, a corporate executive, several former state Teachers-of-the-Year, and about 10 private school teachers who lacked teacher certification. Our philosophy was to hire the best people first and worry about certification later.

To the credit of the state, the New Hampshire Department of Education was flexible enough to respond to a unique set of circumstances and to assemble the necessary certification teams to interview and attest to the competencies of our "alternative" faculty.

As we began to interview applicants, we recognized the complexity of the selection process. We not only had to hire 55 teachers, we had to match personalities and styles. For example, if we hired person X, then person Y was not a good choice. A town resident remarked that he would withhold his judgment as to whether we would be an effective management team until he saw who we let go at the end of year 1 and year 2. This entrepreneur pointed out that start-up companies and their client base grew in stages, while we had to hire a full staff to meet an existing client base of 550 students. It was inevitable that we would make some hiring errors; it remained to be seen, in his eyes, whether we would recognize this and cut our losses. We should note that we did release several teachers after our first year of operation.

We also faced another challenge in hiring. We were hiring for an entrepreneurial enterprise, and it was impossible to gauge an applicant's adaptability to the chaos of a start-up venture. We needed self-starters, decision makers, and people with a high degree of tolerance for ambiguity—qualities that were difficult to discern in a job interview.

That we would be a democratic school was a given, and so we created teacher leaders immediately, asking new hires to develop curriculum, to attend conferences, to write grants, and to organize the 3-week staff orientation in August 1992. Several teachers commented during that orientation that it was difficult to identify the administrators during the training because the leadership changed with each scheduled activity.

In spite of the ardor of the process, it was very fulfilling to watch the school come to a human fruition, manifesting itself in a group of individuals who were deeply committed to a different vision about teaching and learning.

As the challenges of our inaugural year later unfolded, it was clearly the faculty that sold the school to the community. It was this unique set of individuals whose concern about children and the enrichment of learning made parents believers in heterogeneous grouping and new forms of assessment and team teaching. It was the collective energy and dedication and professionalism of this talented group of founding teachers that established a model for educators from around the country to visit, to question, to learn, and ultimately to replicate.

GETTING TO KNOW EACH OTHER

The planning team took a deep breath and realized that we had to stop planning and begin operating a high school.

We all knew that a lot more planning was still needed. At the same time, if the school were to be one where everyone felt a true stake in its evolution, then some key decisions would need to rest with faculty and students. Key to the next steps in the planning process was the willingness and foresight of the school board to give us 3 weeks to meet and plan and bond as a faculty before the start of school. Rather than having the planning team define all of this orientation period, we chose to empower a representative group of the new staff to design the 3 weeks with some parameters as to what things would need to be included.

Having been hired as a charter member of Souhegan's faculty, I (Peggy) was eager to meet my new colleagues and begin the work of creating our school. That work began in August of 1992 during our 3-week orientation. Focused on building relationships, we participated in text-based discussions, performed trust-building exercises, learned how to become advisers to students, decided on definitions of teams, defined Senior Project, learned how to incorporate special educators into heterogeneous classrooms, told stories of our own experiences as students, and laughed at common idiosyncrasies—all the time creating important rituals. We began each day with music and we began and ended each day with a community meeting, all of us sitting in a circle.

Those 3 weeks established a framework for the collegiality we consciously nurtured. In an organization that consciously aims to empower individuals, a spirit of positive negotiations replaces administrative mandates. That spirit was clearly evident in our first community meeting as a new faculty.

We sat in a circle for our first community meeting in August 1992. Community meetings operate in Quaker meeting style: Silence builds between speakers, the topic shifting with each individual speaker. Many topics had been introduced that morning as we all met our colleagues for the first time. Social studies teacher Bags Brokaw broke the silence, cleared his voice, and said, "I don't know how the rest of you feel about this, but I want kids to call me by my first name." His warm voice and friendly smile belied the fact that he had just lobbed an emotional grenade into the crowd. We were, for the most part, teachers who had come from other public schools. We had no context for this suggestion. The forum of this meeting necessitated quiet thought about each topic introduced, however, so the silence built for several minutes while we tried to digest Bag's words. Slowly and carefully, we weighed this idea. Bags had not said what we *should* do, only what he wanted in his relationships with his students. His focus on building relationships in a way that was fundamentally different than most of us had ever experienced in other settings caught our attention. We had all come to Souhegan to forge different relationships with students and with our colleagues, and so after each of us expressed our thoughts, we made our first historic decision as a faculty. Most of us would use our first names in introducing ourselves but would accommodate teachers, students, or parents who were more comfortable in using a more formal address.

That spirit of positive negotiation underscores collegiality. Toward the end of the second trimester in our first year, art teacher Bill Rapf raised his hand at a faculty meeting to ask if anyone would mind changing the master schedule. Snow days had prevented him from completing his course with his students, and he requested that we add a week to the trimester. We all laughed, knowing the traditionally inviolate nature of a school's master schedule. However, after a brief discussion of who or what might be impacted by this change, we voted to change the master schedule, not simply to accommodate the needs of one individual, but to recognize that Bill had voiced a concern that many other teachers shared.

Beyond developing a strong sense of collegiality among our staff, we consciously established systems of space and time that would support close relationships. One small example of this was the architect's design of simple spaces for people to congregate in at the end of each hallway and seating areas next to the front and rear stairways.

The desire to encourage conversation extended to the principal's office as well. In the original design of the school, the principal's office had been placed at the core of the inner sanctum of the main office, far removed from the main corridor. Bob chose to take a smaller office because of its proximity to the central corridor of the school, and asked the architect to cut a door opening directly onto that hall. He created a visible symbol of accessibility, an open door. He lined his desk with juggling equipment and welcomed all visitors as an integral part of his job.

We chose not to organize around department structures, and so we created two teacher workspace areas. These common rooms encourage teachers to develop connections with their peers beyond the boundaries of individual specialties. They also eliminate the "one-room schoolhouse" mentality found in most traditional high schools. The informal conversations in these teacher centers often lead to a new perspective on individual work, and the camaraderie reinforces community.

We have also learned that space and time, while reinforcing the concepts of a personalized culture, can serve as leading indicators of a stressful environment. Open environments need quiet spaces, retreats from constant interaction, and as those quiet spaces become commandeered as classrooms and meeting rooms, we lose the opportunity for the moments of solitude that intense learning demands, both for adults and for students. Increased tension, a by-product of increasing growth and decreasing resources, whittles away at the core concepts of personalization. This is our major concern, as we have grown from an initial population of 550 to close to 1,000 students in just 8 years.

CHAPTER 3

From Mission to Practice

To achieve the kind of world we consider human, some people had to dare to break the thrall of tradition. Next, they had to find ways of recording those new ideas or procedures that improved on what went on before. Finally, they had to find ways of transmitting the new knowledge to the generations to come. (Csikszentmihalyi, 1996, p. 317)

Creating a democratic school proved to be both difficult and exhilarating for a community of more than 700 "citizens." Few precedents existed at the time. This chapter addresses both the philosophy underlying democracy at Souhegan as well as the practices that were put in place to foster and support the emergence of student voices. Other organizational structures, consistent with the beliefs of the Mission Statement and of a democratic culture, were developed and are described here.

In particular, the commitment to a daily Advisory Program became central to the life of the school. In grades 9 and 10, self-contained teams of students and teachers brought both personal support and interdisciplinary thinking to their work together. The last part of this chapter relates the importance of incorporating "inclusion" as a crucial part of the school's belief system and of its practice—a natural outgrowth of an unwavering commitment to heterogeneous grouping.

DEMOCRACY IN ACTION

Our use of space, time, structures, decision making, and traditions deliberately focuses our attention on forging strong interaction among all members of our learning community. With the values of trust and respect as part of the mindset and mission of the school, many of the normal trappings of high school become unnecessary. Since students know how to tell time and since they need to become responsible for their own whereabouts, do we need to ring bells? If we truly trust and respect students, do we need hall passes? Is it necessary for teachers to serve "duty" in the hallways or the cafeteria? If all students are to meet high standards, then does tracking or homogeneous grouping make sense? A belief that students can learn and that they can be trusted and respected leads to self-fulfilling behavior. Students behave in responsible and respectful ways because they are expected to do so.

Perhaps the greatest hypocrisy of American schools is the long-standing pretense that they prepare students to be practicing democratic citizens. Unfortunately, high schools, next to prisons, may be the least democratic institutions in this country. Students are told where to go, what to do, and how to do it; they have little or no voice in schoolwide or classroom decisions. As a consequence, they have little opportunity to practice being thoughtful democratic decision makers. We all recognize that democracy is an extremely messy process, so, too often, we claim it as an adult imperative and deny it to our students.

In designing Souhegan High School, we were aware that a personalized school culture meant a democratic one, a school culture in which students were encouraged to express their views, to speak out if they felt they were not respected or trusted or treated fairly, and to participate in a school governance structure that gave them formal power. The result of our beliefs is our Community Council.

THE COMMUNITY COUNCIL

Souhegan's school governance structure—the Community Council—consists of 45 elected members—25 students and 20 adults who are teachers, staff, administrators, school board members, and residents of Amherst and Mont Vernon. The bylaws of the Community Council state that its purpose is "to govern all school affairs." The Community Council allows student to have a majority voice in key policy decisions. Our Community Council has discussed and decided every single major policy issue since our high school opened in 1992. What we have learned from our experiences in providing a democratic forum is that students will thoughtfully examine serious issues, will solicit a variety of perspectives, will use power wisely, and will vote for the good of the entire school community. The Community Council, with its student majority, has never made a rash or thoughtless decision. Students have always given strong attention to the ways in which a new policy would affect all members of the Souhegan community.

Typically, student councils become the sole vehicles for democracy in action and for making seemingly important decisions, such as when the class trip will take place or whether a soda machine should be installed. In such a context, how can we expect students to become true stakeholders in schools when the only decisions they make are of a perfunctory nature? Unwittingly, we teach them to be passive, dependent, unresponsive, and irresponsible—all those attributes that run counter to the expectations of a democratic citizen.

Development of the Council

Preparing students to understand their role as essential stakeholders required a major investment of time and personnel. When Souhegan first opened, the students, according to faculty representative Sally Houghton, were far more conservative than the adults on the Council. "Students involved in student government are used to being the puppet of the principal. Their involvement is usually limited to the social aspects of school." When dealing with issues of policy, students, like many adults, drift back to their own world of experience, limited by what has always been, not easily drawn to the possibility of what could be.

Paul Schlotman, a teacher who has served on the Community Council since the school's inception, remembers that the students who served on the transition team wanted to impress the adults with their ability to create rules for the new high school. Paul remembers:

> They presented us with a handbook of restrictions and policies for student behavior. They were shocked when I handed their document back to them, telling them that it was a lot of crap. Cleve Penberthy, our first dean of students, challenged them to consider designing rules that everyone would accept, to think about rules in very different ways, to decide that the entire school community would have to endorse a rule before it could become part of our culture. Cleve presented his ideas of a behavior code to the Community Council for their endorsement; after conversation and revision, this document became our community's rules.

The Souhegan Six

1. Respect and encourage the right to teach and the right to learn at all times.
2. Be actively engaged in the learning; ask questions, collaborate, and seek solutions.
3. Be on time to fulfill your daily commitments.

4. Be appropriate; demonstrate behavior that is considerate of the community, the campus, and yourself.
5. Be truthful; communicate honestly.
6. Be responsible and accountable for your choices.

Implications of Council Participation

Paul Schlotman believes that the conversation is more important than the results, that the Council's most important role is to serve as an educational forum. As students and adults grappled with forming a structure, they were educating themselves in the democratic process. One of the first decisions made was to give kids the majority of seats on the Council. According to Paul, "Often, an adult can swing the conversation in a certain way; it is essential that students have more peers with whom to weigh an issue. The success of the Community Council depends on the quality of the adults. The adults can never lose sight of their role in this forum."

To ensure that the Community Council represented the diverse voices of the student body, we developed an at-large representation, five students who would be appointed by the Council. The intent was to have them represent a constituency of disenfranchised students who would offer a perspective not usually evident in traditional student councils. According to Paul:

> These kids made a difference when we were trying to get this organization up and running. One kid was a constant truant, and our physics teacher chased this kid all year, eventually changing the way this kid thought about education. The kid said that no teacher had ever wanted him in a classroom before, and he had just been marking time, waiting to drop out. The following year, he sought to become part of Community Council, stating that he was one of the 10% of the kids causing 90% of the problems. He represented a whole group of kids, and we did not want to exclude that group. We couldn't if we wanted this thing to fly, if we wanted kids to become full stakeholders in their school. These kids are the barometers of the school.

One former member, Dan Ward ('00), agrees with Paul. In and out of trouble during his first 2 years at Souhegan, Dan says:

> Once I was able to behave responsibly, I was elected to the Community Council. As somebody who had experienced a lot of disciplinary actions, I wanted to make sure that discipline was

enacted in an even manner. I wanted everyone to understand that we need to live by the Mission Statement here at school. Without it, we are just another school.

Dan highlights student awareness of the Mission Statement as the foundation document of the school and its policies. Two Council members addressed this need to retain the Mission Statement as the central focus of all school policies. Kerry Silva ('98) and John Coakley ('98) proposed that anyone submitting a proposal to the Council first demonstrate how their ideas would link to the Mission Statement and then demonstrate that the proposal was supported by a group of people. This idea would sustain the focus on the central mission of the school and eliminate nonsensical proposals.

Sample of Issues Considered

Parking. Our students learned quickly how to translate democratic theory into practice. Parking issues loomed large in the first year of the school, and the Community Council entertained a proposal for a senior parking lot. When the Council opposed the idea of creating a privileged group, the author of the proposal stated that a precedent had already been set when the faculty had received preferential parking privileges. The Council then voted to eliminate the faculty privilege. After a few weeks, members of the faculty appealed this decision. The senior who had begun this debate linked his senior parking to the proposal to assign faculty spots. It passed, with the senior commenting that he had just ridden the wave to getting what he had wanted all along. These early skirmishes established the Council as the policy-making governance board of the school.

Smoking. One significant issue brought before the Community Council was the elimination of the outdoor smoking pit, created for students over 18 and for adults. Although its presence had always been controversial, the rationale had been to prevent smoking in the new building. According to faculty representative Michael Facques:

It accomplished that purpose, but its presence was in complete contrast with the health and wellness concerns of the school's mission. It also caused enforcement issues and was a constant public relations nightmare as students from the middle school, located about 100 yards from Souhegan, began to use the area.

The Community Council did its homework on the issue, developing petitions, surveying constituents, and enlisting the help of Alan Gordon, the school's drug and alcohol counselor. The Council decided to hold its vote at night so that parents and members of the community might attend and participate in the debate. Member Bob Quay ('99) was dismayed when Dr. Bob Mackin used the PA system to lobby for his perspective to the entire school community on the afternoon of the debate. Bob Quay stated:

> The vote was scheduled for that evening, and the forum for the debate was the meeting. Dr. Bob could not attend that night, and so he decided to broadcast his views to the entire school. This was not appropriate because he was using a medium that only he had access to, thereby bringing the debate outside the forum. I spoke to him about this, and he permitted me to broadcast my opposing views to the school. Although I am not a smoker, I believed that the elimination of the smoking pit infringed on individual rights. However, I wanted the debate to be contained within the forum designed to address the issue.

Dr. Bob's response to Bob Quay underscored his recognition of the issue of fairness. Had the principal denied this student's request for equal access to a key communication medium, he would have seriously jeopardized a valuable exercise in the democratic process.

The meeting was well attended. Students, parents, and faculty members addressed the Council. One student smoker spoke in favor of eliminating the pit. He believed that its presence spurred his addiction, providing a "cool" place for him to hang out with older kids. His testimony underscored the value of providing a forum for wrestling with tough issues. The Council voted to eliminate the smoking pit and ban smoking on campus. Michael Facques says:

> We could have chosen to do nothing. The state planned to outlaw smoking on school property within a year anyway, but we decided to bring it to our voters. This issue provided an opportunity to develop leadership within the Community Council and to provide a platform for discourse. It was important to consider a decision that would affect many students.

Modified Block Schedule. Community Council works best when addressing issues of concern to the entire school. Michael Facques believes that "we teach democracy by modeling it. Democracy has never been a spectator sport." The most significant issue addressed by Community Council since the school's opening was the debate, in 1995, on adopting a modified block schedule. Until this point, class periods were 55 minutes long; the only variation of this schedule existed for ninth- and tenth-grade teams who designed their own schedules within an extended block of time. Several faculty members had researched different scheduling options and presented them to the faculty for approval. The faculty members of Community Council reminded their colleagues that the proposal would have to be passed by the Community Council before we could adopt it as policy. There was serious opposition to this among the faculty. Some teachers believed that this issue needed to be decided by educators; they did not believe that students would understand the positive impact of a flexible schedule.

Preliminary conversations among students confirmed the teachers' perspective. Council representatives polled each Advisory and reported almost unanimous negative feedback from younger students, despite the fact that the majority of teachers were in support of the proposed schedule. The school was polarized. Rather than limiting the decision making to the Council, as had been the traditional pattern, student representative Bob Quay ('97) and faculty representative Mike Beliveau proposed that the Council sponsor a town meeting for the entire school community. The entire school would then vote to recommend adoption or rejection of the block-schedule proposal; this vote would be binding. The day before this forum, faculty members again expressed their dismay that such an important issue was being left to students. Several predicted that the students would overwhelmingly reject the block-scheduling proposal.

The Council assembled ninth- and twelfth-grade students and faculty for the first open-mike assembly and tenth- and eleventh-grade students and faculty for the second round. The younger students expressed their concerns at the possibility of having to spend more time in beginning-level language classes and in math classes, two difficult classes in a block-schedule environment. Juniors and seniors listened to their peers, then encouraged them to take a longer view of the possibilities inherent in a different schedule. Many spoke of the additional time given for science labs or to use the school's technology. Many students spoke of the pleasure of having a 2-hour free period once a week to work or being able to leave campus for a long lunch break. They urged freshmen and sophomores to think beyond their immediate experience, to consider the greater good. Teachers acknowledged to the students that they planned to work with each other to prepare for teaching in longer blocks of time. The atmosphere during both sessions was respectful as kids and teachers questioned each other and listened to each other. At the end of the town meeting, the school community voted by secret ballot. At the end of the day, the Community Council announced that 85% had voted in favor of the block-scheduling proposal.

Food and Drink in the Classrooms. In the winter of 2001, the Community Council led the school through a debate about the merits of allowing food and drink in classrooms and other carpeted areas of the school. This issue has been raised every year in many conversations, arguments, and proposals before the Council. At the end of a very lengthy process, the Council deliberated on the issue, and the Council, made up of a majority of students, decided that students had not earned the privilege of eating food and drink on the carpeted areas.

Their vote *not* to allow food and drink surprised everyone. Council adviser Michael Facques, in an e-mail message to the faculty following the vote, stated that the process was a major indicator that students took the concepts of the Mission Statement very seriously. He urged his colleagues to support their efforts.

> This is another example of the members of the Council being willing to step up and put the good of the school ahead of their own individual interests. We need to put our own interests aside to support the work of the Council and the belief in the Mission Statement's call for respect and trust in our community.

Michael proposed bringing before the Council a proposal to allow for faculty and staff to eat and drink on the carpet. Stating that being fair did not always mean being equal, Michael invited colleagues to discuss this idea.

Ted Hall, who succeeded Bob Mackin as Souhegan's principal in June 1998, also underscored the need for adults to enforce the Council's vote if the Council were to maintain their credibility as a policy-making board.

The faculty and staff were very quick to signal their support. In e-mail replies, they promised to put aside personal interests in favor of the public good. Most agreed that a proposal to allow faculty more flexibility was a good idea. One respondent pointed out that the difference would demonstrate that positive behaviors result in positive change. Another, however, cautioned Michael to proceed slowly, that creating different rules for adults and students would create difficulties throughout the building. In their responses, adult members of the Souhegan community validated the continued belief in democratic governance.

Issues Not Considered

Accelerated Courses. Some issues have not been appropriate for Community Council involvement. One student member proposed a fundamental change to the school's heterogeneous culture. His proposal called for an accelerated level of courses, open to everyone motivated to succeed in rigorous coursework. The Council questioned whether his proposal reflected the views of his constituents or whether they represented only his perspective. They suggested that he set up a series of meetings with other students, teachers, and administrators before the Council considered his proposal. Upon investigation, he came to recognize the responsibility and obligation of the faculty to direct the education of the students. He learned that the issues he had raised were being addressed by other groups, and he withdrew his proposal.

Faculty representative Sally Houghton admits to a high degree of emotion during the debate on the merits of accelerated classes:

> I stalked out of one meeting, insulted by several remarks of two students, but in the end, we figured it out. Although withdrawing this proposal was the right thing to do, the entire debate underscored for me a rising change in the makeup of the Council. We no longer have members who represent the fringe groups of the school, and without those voices, we lose a valuable component in our debates and risk becoming elitist in our actions. We need to continually invite participation by those who do not traditionally participate in school issues.

Homework over Vacations. Principal Ted Hall told the faculty that he planned to ask the Community Council to develop a policy regarding homework assignments over vacations. Some teachers expressed strong feelings that the Council had no right to interfere with their autonomy. The ensuing conversation demonstrated clearly that the rapid growth of both our student and faculty population has contributed to a lack of institutional memory. This lack threatens the organization that is the cornerstone of our democratic school. Faculty representative Michael Facques states:

> Faculty members sometimes fear their lack of voice in the Council. They forget that there are faculty members and staff members and community members on the Council, not just students. Another issue is that we have many new staff members who were not here to witness the Council's leadership of powerful initiatives.

The Council has not pushed the proposal to study the assignment of homework over vacations, shying away from what is sure to be a highly charged conversation on an issue that inspires passion among many. Students often become pawns in the competing viewpoints of teachers who set academic priorities and families who want to spend time with their children without academic consequences. Added to this mix are athletic coaches who set sports schedules, theater directors who set rehearsal times, and employers who set work hours. All make compelling arguments about structuring time. The Community Council would provide a forum for substantial conversation about this universal, provocative issue.

The faculty representatives would like to see the Council tackle the issue. As Michael Facques states:

> The homework issue is a classic one for Community Council to discuss. Similar to block scheduling, it affects every single constituency in the school. Structured conversation is valuable. We should hear parents' thoughts on the impact on family life, and teachers' thoughts on the impact of academic rigor, and students' thoughts on their own needs. We should not shy away from it. Let's grapple with it. Let's sell it; let's convince each other.

The Opportunity to Make a Difference

In order to promote the participation of a diverse group of students, adults in the school community need to recognize the importance of student voice in decision making. Adults are the constant in a school community; the student population is constantly changing. Without a consistent adult investment, students stumble.

Each year the Council sponsors a day-long retreat for its members. The goal of the retreat is to provide a focus for the work of the Council and to develop the leadership potential of the group. In January 2000, only three adult members of the Council were present, demonstrating the constant tension in scheduling time that is convenient for both students and adults.

The conversation among the students demonstrated their intent to improve the school environment through increased communication, active participation, and their increased visibility as student leaders. They wanted to leave a legacy of having made a difference. They needed more adult witnesses for their intentions, and they will need the counsel of adult guides to help them accomplish their goals.

Former dean of students Bags Brokaw applauds what he calls "democracy by the seat of our pants." He states:

> Schools are social and cultural institutions as well as academic institutions. Bringing forth the principles of democratic and just counsel requires listening for the teachable moments. In an anti-hierarchichal culture, role models take on incredible importance. Kids learn best when given matters of substance to debate, a respect-

ful environment in which to learn, and the opportunity to make a difference. At Souhegan, our Mission Statement provides our core beliefs, the Souhegan Six provides the behavioral norms, Advisory groups provide a means to disseminate ideas based on our beliefs, and the Community Council provides the structure for developing the big ideas confronting us.

Whole-school conversations about issues of concern to students and adults offer a catalyst for reflection, debate, and action. Leadership and consistent affirmation of the tenets of democracy are essential components in producing an active citizenry. Michael Facques believes:

> If we create and sustain a democratic culture at school, we create and sustain a lifelong interest in involvement in local and national issues. Students who have a voice and a vote in their school will, hopefully, exercise their voice and their vote as adults.

Much like the efforts we see in corporate cultures to empower employees, schools, too, can empower students to feel a human stake in a democratic community.

SUPPORTING STUDENT ENGAGEMENT

Organizational Structures

From an organizational standpoint, we chose to design structures and policies for the 95% of students who would take the concept of "community of learners" to heart. All schools inevitably deal with the 5% who challenge the boundaries, but we believed that even that number shrinks when a premium is placed on individual responsibility.

Most decisions are made by the people who need to make them. For instance, we have seven daily schedules in our schoolday. The master schedule lists the start and end times for Division Two classes (grades 11 and 12) and elective courses for grades 9 and 10. This schedule contains six academic periods of 55 minutes each and a lunch/Advisory block. The master schedule also includes modified blocks on 2 days of the week. Each of the three teams at grades 9 and 10 have a large block of time and the flexibility to design schedules to meet curricular needs.

Our organizational structure is relatively flat. We have a principal, two deans of faculty, and a dean of students. We also have departmental coordinators, who receive a small stipend for their work and in some cases a slightly reduced teaching schedule, but their role is not supervisory or evaluative. We also offer stipends to teachers who assume various forms of leadership in the school, for example, those who coordinate our Senior Project, our Division One Exhibition, our Graduate Intern Program, and so forth.

All adults in our building support student engagement. Our support staff provides the backbone to the school, often extending their work to include serving as advisers, coaches of extracurricular or team sports, and mentors to Senior Projects. Jim Rines, our facilities manager, coaches girls' softball and junior varsity girls' field hockey, once paying off a bet with his team by wearing a skirt to work. Attendance secretary Lynda Conley serves as a surrogate parent to many kids who need a touchstone throughout their schoolday. She says, "Earning my trust seems to matter to some kids who are not typically at their best in the classroom. They want me to be proud of them, and I am."

Strengthening the bonds between the student and the adult members of our school community requires attention to both informal and formal rituals and traditions. Terrence Deal and Allen Kennedy (1982) have stated that "in the absence of ceremony or ritual, important values have no impact" (p. 63). The specifics of these events are not as important as the message they send to all members of the school community. When a ninth-grade Advisory sought support for a schoolwide fundraiser for cancer research, the school responded by raising over $5,000 through a sponsored race called the "Run for Hope." Classes were shortened for the day, and everyone turned out for the schoolwide barbecue and fun-run. What is significant about this event is that teacher Amy Pham and her students assumed that in a school built upon trust and respect, they would gain support from students, faculty, and administrators who would work together for the day's success. Adults encourage students to develop leadership skills; therefore, the mindset of the community presumes that good ideas will find support.

When information specialist Kim Carter wanted to explore the question of why some students lose interest in their studies, Bob Mackin suggested that she propose a pilot course. Kim created a course called Carpe Diem, even though Nancy Baker told her that, contrary to popular belief, the correct translation of that phrase means "to pluck the day." Figuring that that metaphor would work just as well, Kim kept the title. She discusses her decision to create this course:

> The thought of designing a course for kids who don't like courses was somewhat of an oxymoron, but I was intrigued by the possibilities presented to me. My relationships with two particular students and my humbling awareness that the system did not

work for my own two children, led me to question whether any system of public education could engage and challenge every student, or at least students whose own passions for particular interests and styles of learning required more flexibility than a traditional course of study.

The idea of adult mentorship of individual student interest formed the basis of this course. Students would choose an idea that interested them, present a proposal for their work to a group of adults, and earn credit for a completed body of work. When I met with the kids, we realized that we did not all share a common opening in our schedules, so we created an Advisory that would offer an elective credit as well.

After exploring their individual learning styles, Bloom's taxonomy, and a structure for the learning cycle, the students developed proposals for the diverse ideas they wanted to pursue. One girl wanted to compose her own music and create a music video, learning video production techniques as well. Two other students worked collaboratively on developing a Web page for the physics instructor. One student set out to define his own life philosophy, while another planned to learn Hebrew before a trip to Israel.

I pulled in counselors, teachers, and administrators to sit as reviewers as the students presented their proposals for the work they would do during our Advisory time, modifying one of our Critical Friends Group protocols for the process. The adults posed valuable questions to the students. One of our deans of faculty offered to collaborate with one student who wanted to study the school's Honors Program. In critiquing the proposals, students found that the most significant and insightful feedback often came from their peers.

Everything I do at Souhegan springs from our Mission Statement. My work on this course allowed me the time to explore the question of how we can provide both structure and flexibility to maximize learning for all students.

Learning Expectations

"We all came here," says dean of faculty Jim Bosman, "because we wanted to change the patterns of teaching and learning, and we have done that." A jazzy curriculum does not ensure student learning. We ask students to demonstrate their progress in specific learning expectations originally developed by Robert Marzano (1994) and modified and adopted by our staff. We expect students to demonstrate their progress in becoming

Knowledgeable persons
Complex thinkers
Effective communicators
Skilled information processors
Self-directed learners
Collaborative workers
Responsible citizens

We ask students to move beyond mere seat time as a way of accumulating credits. Students are asked to demonstrate their learning and to apply that learning through a variety of requirements. Souhegan's graduation requirements meet, and in many cases exceed, the state of New Hampshire's requirements. Souhegan requires that all students accumulate 22.5 credits, including 3 credits each in math, science, and social studies. Students must also complete 40 hours of community service, participate in 4 years of Advisory, and pass three performance-based assessments: the Division One Exhibition (see Chapter 4), the Junior Research Paper, and the Senior Project (see Chapter 4).

We believe that in order to demonstrate basic knowledge and skills, students must earn at least a C– in a course. We do not award a passing grade lower than a C–. Students who have not met the basic criteria are given no credit (NC) and must make up the credit.

Students are presented with the opportunity to earn honors designation in their courses by fulfilling the Honors Challenge contract and receiving a grade of B or better in their coursework. Honors Challenges may include participation in Socratic Seminars, alternative assignments, different book choices, and so forth. Honors Challenges do not imply more work, but rather work requiring a different level of engagement. Honors are awarded at the end of the course of study, once students have demonstrated that they have earned this designation. Students who do not complete the Honors Challenges in a course, but accomplish work of sufficient quality, may be awarded "academic distinction."

Our students are not offered a wide palette of courses. We believe that there are specific skills and content, a core curriculum, that students must master to receive a diploma from Souhegan High School. Our students all spend 2 years studying American history and literature and the foundations of a democratic society. All students take the same integrated math courses in ninth and tenth grades. All students take the same science courses in their first 2 years of high school to provide them with a strong foundation for further study. As juniors, all students take a 2-credit World Studies course to broaden their awareness of global relationships.

The Foundations of Classroom Practice

The question all schools face, regardless of philosophy, is how to facilitate the relationship between the learner and what is to be learned. An authentic curriculum creates essential links between learning and application, a link seldom forged through a textbook; rather, it bursts forth in the human connection between student and teacher. For classics teacher Nancy Baker, this connection occurs at a specific moment.

> I have learned that the most important part of any assignment is the middle. I set the task and I assess it, but in the middle is the shared responsibility. The middle is the place that student work improves. There is time to make it better. This is the point of any work at which the students acknowledge what they do not know; the teacher becomes a coach of their learning. This middle point is the moment of the greatest power in terms of student learning.

The blueprint for that level of authenticity is as different as each teacher, each subject, each student, and each setting, but there are commonalities in the scaffolds we have put in place:

- We focus on essential questions rather than textbooks.
- We focus on authentic contexts for our curriculum.
- We focus on performance-based assessments.
- We focus on including all students in our curriculum.
- We offer Honors designations to students in every classroom.
- We focus on collaboration with our peers.
- We focus on reflection in our daily practice.
- We focus on involving colleagues in our work.

We have strong supports for the work we aspire to do each day. We also recognize that we are human and that we sometimes fall short of our aspirations.

Authentic relationships with teacher mentors and coaches foster authentic learning for students. Learning becomes more than a paper-and-pencil exercise; it becomes a human dynamic where teachers confidently call upon students to become workers and to demonstrate publicly, in front of both faculty and student peers, that they truly know something. Acquiring the ease and skill to perform or exhibit in regular and routine ways is a direct result of feeling cared for and supported. As Allison Rowe,

Souhegan's first dean of faculty, once said, "New norms of achievement result from new norms of respect and trust."

This intense blend of a highly task-focused school that pushes students continually to "expand their comfortable limits" and an atmosphere that is almost compulsively humane and deeply personalized is ultimately what sets Souhegan apart from many other high schools. 1996 graduate Courtney Banghart believes that "if we were to do a survey of all Souhegan graduates, we would probably discover that a very high percentage of them become teachers. We learned a lot about personal mission at Souhegan, and that spirit breeds teachers—even in this age of dot-com wealth."

Learning about personal mission is not left to chance. In the next section, members of the Souhegan community discuss their participation in our daily Advisory program, the place where we make our values explicit to our students.

ADVISORY

When Souhegan first opened in 1992, the focus on personalization was not entirely popular. Amid the publicity and political hoopla surrounding the Goals 2000 reform efforts started in the early 1990s, the whole idea of personalization of high schools had taken on an almost negative connotation. Conservative groups in many communities around the country attempted to convince both parents and educators that concepts such as self-esteem or human tolerance should not be the province of schools.

In our view, such efforts to downplay the human side of schooling were missing the mark. In spite of the reticence—and in some cases the outright hostility of certain parents and community members—we consciously strove to create a collaborative community. While the voices of our adversaries were loud ones, we were also being told by corporate and business leaders that they wanted employees who were able to work in teams, to communicate effectively, to exhibit strong personal and interpersonal skills, to be adaptable to change, and to know *how* to learn. These were viewed as the essential attributes for the new corporate culture and ultimately for competing globally in the 21st century.

With that in mind, Souhegan, like many schools today, took on a more holistic mission than that suggested by "back-to-basics" reform advocates. It is a mission that called for basic proficiency in a broad range of personal and interpersonal skills in addition to the basic academic learning proficiencies we all recognize are required. And it is a mission that can best be accomplished within a humane and personalized setting.

We strive to give our students the academic skills they will need to succeed in their future, while also strengthening the personal bonds between adolescents and adults. Greatly influenced by Ted Sizer's work and the Common Principles of the Coalition of Essential Schools, we believed that the presence of caring adults in students' lives would lead to greater success for each child. We knew, therefore, that we had to provide the time and opportunity to get to know our students well. Our daily Advisory Program brings together ten students and one adult each day, to ensure that each child in our school has an adult advocate. This advocacy role takes on many forms over the 4 years of high school. Ninth-grade advisers focus attention on transition issues and breaking down social stereotypes, tenth-grade advisers mentor the Division One Exhibition (see Chapter 4), eleventh-grade advisers help students map out their postsecondary plans, and twelfth-grade advisers monitor student progress in their Senior Project (see Chapter 4).

The Purpose of Advisory

Our Program of Studies states that Advisory is a daily meeting with 10 to 12 students and a staff adviser who provides academic and personal support and helps foster communication skills, team building, trust, and individual self-esteem. The adviser becomes a primary contact person with parents, students, and teachers. Successful completion of 4 years of Advisory is required for graduation. Advisories meet each day for 25 minutes, before or after lunch.

There is more to Advisory than this definition provides. First and foremost, our Advisory Program is the result of our conscious and deliberate decision to ensure that each child in our school has an adult advocate. Our Mission Statement calls upon us "to challenge and expand the comfortable limits of thought, tolerance, and performance." Advisory is the place where much of that happens, where the Mission Statement is implemented on a daily basis. Guidance counselor Alan Gordon, who played a major role in the implementation of our Advisory Program, offers these thoughts:

> I listened carefully to Cleve Penberthy, our first dean of students, describe how at most schools students arrive every morning and drop off their hearts, bodies, and souls outside the front door. Their heads come into school for about 7 hours and then rejoin the other parts of themselves outside, at the end of the day. Cleve intended that at Souhegan we would do things differently; whole persons would enter our school to engage in the business of learning every day.

Personalization became one of a very few essential primary building blocks on which Souhegan High School was constructed.

When we began our work together in August of 1992, our orientation activities underscored many of the tasks essential to creating a strong Advisory Program. We needed to establish a supportive professional community. We needed to create a place where a heterogeneous group of adults and young people would feel comfortable enough to engage in the business of learning.

We needed to involve ourselves in team-building activities that would quickly form us into closely knit faculty. We needed to discover ways in which to integrate the Mission Statement into our daily school lives. These goals were identical to those that advisers face on entering their new Advisories every year.

The skills involved in running a good Advisory are the very same that are involved in teaching a good class. They can be taught. Advisers need to feel comfortable interacting informally with students. They need to know how to ask open-ended questions. They need to know how to facilitate a good discussion. They need to learn debriefing skills. The application of debriefing skills provides the opportunity for a group to examine its own progress. It jump-starts the group process on a regular basis. When we examine how we are doing as a group, we begin to share responsibility for the development of that group. Ownership of the group can begin to be shared among advisees and advisers.

One important aspect of Advisory is crisis intervention. Following a fatal car accident involving students at my daughter's school, an announcement was made at the end of the day; kids were sent home in tears with no school-based adult to talk to. We need to ensure that nothing like this ever happens at Souhegan High School. Here, in the event of a crisis, students and staff go immediately to Advisory to hear or read a common announcement. We take time out to react in a safe, comfortable setting. We identify students who might be at risk due to the nature of the news we have just heard. We believe that the event, and what can be learned from it, is so important that giving time and attention to it supersedes any preplanned classroom curriculum.

We often use metaphors to describe Advisory to parents. We sometimes think of Advisory as a carpool, where kids allow adults to overhear their casual conversation. Occasionally, the driver can interject a point of view or change the focus of the conversation, but the driver does not "own" the carpool. Advisory can also parallel a family dinner table, where conversations can vary from the provocative to the "pass the salt" variety. It is the aggregate of all those dinners that forms the story of the family. And sometimes, Advisory mimics life in a fire station—a lot of time is spent on maintenance, but when a fire breaks out, the engine is ready to respond.

Student Views. Students understand the purpose of Advisory and are eager to share their views. More than 400 students responded within 2 days to our survey of their thoughts on the purpose of Advisory. These responses are typical of those received:

Molly Blessing ('00): Advisory "gives kids and teachers time to get together to support each other's ideas and thoughts."

Nick Neverisky ('02): "Advisory is about camaraderie. That, and pizza, you can't forget about pizza. Advisory means a great deal to me. . . . It has given me the opportunity to get to know my classmates, teachers, and myself."

Emily Bielagus ('02): "It's hard to go unnoticed in an environment where every student's feelings are considered and discussed."

Ben Meade ('02): "The meaning of Advisory is to have a person-to-person relationship, not a student-to-faculty relationship."

Josh Robinson ('02): "When I moved to Amherst at the start of ninth grade, for a fellow member of my Advisory to say hello to me in the halls . . . was a good feeling . . . it was a way to meet people."

Jaime Lefkowitz ('02): "Advisory offers a break from school work to talk and share opinions. Sometimes Advisory brings out qualities in people who might otherwise be in shadow. This lets us gain respect for each other, to realize our differences, and most of all, to respect them."

All of the respondents used similar words to convey the meaning of Advisory: comfort, support, relaxed setting, bonding, security, trust, reflection, a sense of belonging.

Special relationships with adult advisers matter to kids. Jaimie Harrow ('03) appreciates that "there is always a teacher looking after the welfare of a student." Judson Irish ('03) knows that "if someone does mess up, then the adviser is always there to help. " Junior Chris Vassallo believes that "if Columbine could not be prevented, it could definitely be predicted. Advisers seem to get to know their kids fairly well, and if something was disturbing one of them, they would be able to tell." Samantha Allen ('02) credits her adviser with "always pushing me to do better in classes. She wants me to get all that I can out of the classes I take, and it's important to have an adult in school backing and pushing you all the way." One student remembers the day we learned about the death of a classmate. Her adviser "had been crying for quite some time. Our whole Advisory sat on the floor in the hall and talked about what had happened. I don't think that there was a dry eye that day."

Students understand the collegial nature of Advisory. Dan Cronin ('98) offered to facilitate his ninth-grade Advisory through a difficult conflict they were experiencing. John MacDonald ('02) speaks of "creating bonds that strengthen the community. Advisory matters to me, every day in Advisory matters to me." Senior Christopher Wason "likes to sit around and share stories. It is a very special thing when an Advisory works. It needs to have all the elements to work, and it needs to be a group effort."

Faculty Views. The two teachers who work with a student with autism find that Advisory "gives an excellent opportunity for this student to interact with peers in a casual environment and also for other students to learn more about autism."

Theater teacher Steve Hodgman found the first couple of years of Advisory difficult:

> As a committed optimist, I wanted all students to get along all of the time. That hadn't happened, of course. But then, one group just clicked. They hugged a lot, brought food a lot, even organized projects at the local soup kitchen. We decided to travel to New York City together, staying at an apartment owned by a relative of one of my advisees. I brought my family along, and everybody took turns looking after my kids.
>
> The remarkable thing is that this group was no different from any other group I had had; they were a combination of overachievers, underachievers, athletes, actors—they just liked each other's company.

Art teacher Martha Rives learned that her sense of Advisory identity relates to the students' role in setting the tone. She finds that "kids invest in Advisory as a place where they learn about problem solving and personal responsibility if they tie themselves to standards of behavior and participation that they design with their Adviser."

After attending a weekend training session for a Peer Outreach program, Chip Bailey found a link to his work with his Advisory. "I understood more clearly the forces in the lives of students. I accepted my advisees for who they were, was honest with them, and confronted them when needed."

For Advisory to function well, we all search for ways to form a cohesive bond with widely diverse students. As a way of underscoring the need for participation, Kris Gallo asked her first Advisory to design an effort rubric. When she mentioned the value of participating in discussion, Carl pointed out that not talking did not mean not listening. He said that every group needs people who will listen. "I do not tune out," he said, "I listen."

Outcomes

We believe in the cumulative effect of creating a caring community. We reinforce our beliefs every single day in a dedicated period of time devoted to knowing a small group of individuals well. We know that this makes a difference in students' lives.

Sometimes, however, we believe in Advisory as an ideal, not as the place we most want to be on a particular day. Sometimes teachers groan as they leave the lunch table, hoping that a fire drill might cancel Advisory for the day. We whine and drag our feet, and, of course, sometimes our students whine as well: "Why can't we go outside/stay inside? . . . Why do we always/never play games? . . . I don't want to have an academic day. . . . Why do you always nag me about_____. . . . How come we never/always do what so-and-so does in his Advisory? . . . I gotta go find somebody. . . . I'm bored. . . . This Advisory is boring. . . . We never do anything. . . . How come we always gotta talk? . . . Please can I go ask somebody something—I'll only be a minute, I swear. . . . It's so lame. . . . Nobody ever wants to do what I want. . . . Why do we always have to sit in a circle?"

Whining about Advisory is one of those "cheesy-bonding" experiences that one graduate urged us to continue. Her phrase became part of the Souhegan vocabulary.

The cheesy bonding in Advisory forces interaction between every member of every social, academic, and athletic clique in the school. Every day for 25 minutes, Metallica meets Jewel, Marilyn Manson meets 'N Sync, and even if the sole thing that happens during that 25 minutes is that the most popular student in the tenth grade plays Pictionary with the most disenfranchised student in the tenth grade, that is a good and worthy investment of time. There is much to separate our children in their worlds; Advisory promotes a connection beyond their usual and customary definition of themselves. That connection is vital in the development of a democratic society; it is as worthy as any academic endeavor in any classroom.

Risky business, this stuff. In order for Advisory to make a difference, we need to respect each other's vulnerability and volatility, and that requires constant attention. We ask students to honor the confidential nature of Advisory, not to exclude any stakeholders in a child's safety and well-being, but to ensure that conversations in Advisory do not continue as gossip in the hallway. Alan Gordon believes:

It is important to note that we adults do not create or promote these conversations. They take place in the bathrooms, hallways, and parking lots all the time. Kids talk about parties, about drinking too much, about dieting, about sleeping together, about drugs, about pregnancy, about Web sites that produce term papers, about cheating on a physics midterm, about their church youth groups, about how to apply to college, about finding a job, about whether to get a tattoo. If we are successful and fortunate, kids will trust us enough to bring those conversations into Advisory. That gives us an opportunity to inject into the conversation timely thoughts and suggestions and to create teachable moments. We do not purposely invade the private space of students and their families. Advisers are not trained psychologists or counselors; they are merely good listeners. If we create a secure safety net for students' feelings, they will often share those feelings and raw emotions with us. And thank God they do.

Raw emotions vary, of course, in an adolescent population. Confidentiality allowed one ninth-grader, Josh, to talk about the crush he had on a girl he had met at his orthodontist's office. He wanted to find out more about her, and maybe even call her, but he didn't know how to proceed. A couple of kids role-played conversations with Josh, and then he practiced what he would say to her when he did call. Everybody insisted that Josh report back to the Advisory, surrounding that event with gentle laughter. Josh's privacy was maintained because nobody talked about his dilemma outside of Advisory.

Lisa used her ninth-grade Advisory to vent about how unfair her mother was about a curfew on prom night. Her adviser tried to get her to see that her mother was concerned for her safety as a 14-year-old in the company of 18- and 19-year-olds. She was furious, because "everybody knows you don't do 'IT' until sophomore year!" Other kids in the Advisory nodded their heads, agreeing with that informal commandment about losing one's virginity. The stunned adviser used that conversation to begin a sustained discussion of sexual mores. The adviser maintained Lisa's confidentiality but shared the outline of the ensuing discussion with other advisers and the school nurse as an opportunity to open communication with other Advisories.

A student in Jess Tremblay's Advisory routinely asked her to "tell me something good about myself; I need to hear it right now." A troubled boy, silent and disengaged in class, he eventually began to connect with others in his Advisory when he realized that some of them also had a lot of difficulty with some coursework.

Recognizing the raw emotions of one student experiencing a crisis, adviser Mike Beliveau invited him to spend time with Mike's family, hoping to provide him a sense of grounding during a tumultuous time.

Support for Advisers

Advisory raises many questions for which there are no right answers. What happens if a student confides that he has no faith in one of his teachers? How does an Advisory handle the information that an advisee's friend is vomiting every day after lunch? Is it okay for an adviser to share her own experience about a date rape when an advisee opens that topic for discussion? How can we engage in a conversation about drinking that goes beyond preaching to a bored audience? What do we do when asked about our own drinking? Who can help change the dynamics of a troubled group? How do we include a strange new member? How do we deal with two subgroups that have developed? What if the group doesn't want to do anything at all?

We bring those questions to grade-level Advisory meetings, facilitated by Alan Gordon. At best, these meetings serve as a sort of adult Advisory, providing an opportunity for us to support one another, offer suggestions, and reassure one another that we are not alone. We raise difficult questions to gain support for our individual experiences. We discuss common grade-level themes and curriculum. We search for solutions for the truly wrenching topics of destructive behaviors that some of our students wrestle with. We talk; we talk constantly. Without sustained time to talk and reflect on our work in this powerful arena, Advisory would fail; powerful connections require powerful investments.

The training we receive helps us to understand that there are three major categories that students might bring to us, as advisers or teachers:

- *Problems* are the issues of everyday adolescence: relationships, academic difficulties, uncertainty about future plans, and so forth.
- *Crises* are issues on which we need to consult with each other or a counselor: divorce, eating disorders, substance abuse, death and dying, pregnancy, and so forth.
- *Emergencies* require an immediate referral to the student's counselor: threats of suicide or homicide, abuse, rape, and so forth.

Advisers and teachers consult with our counseling staff for help with difficult issues.

The composition of any single group impacts the nature of that Advisory, according to Alan Gordon:

The challenge thus becomes the identification of those features all Advisories share in common. It is not curriculum, because the curriculum of Advisory is really the experiences, interests, values, skills, hopes, and fears of all the individual members. It boils down to skills and process. Students learn the skills and develop the ability to function in a heterogeneous group of their peers. They learn how to listen, facilitate, lead, cooperate, care, and support. Most of this learning occurs indirectly during the meals, games, and discussions that take place. Occasionally, effective debriefing makes that learning more directly evident. We draw upon that learning on a daily basis in the classroom and much less frequently during a crisis.

The best advisers are the best teachers. The best advisers are the people who are able to be natural and comfortable with a group of kids, individuals who can ask an open-ended question and facilitate a discussion, and train their kids to do that.

Alan is "afraid that the more we 'curricularize' Advisory, the more we compromise the fragile nature of that safety net." Rich Wallace (Wally) shares this struggle:

> As an adviser, I have been able to refer, advocate, and, most importantly, intervene. Being able to listen is the most important skill we can employ as an adviser. We need to approach Advisory as a time when the adviser may be the only adult in a student's life who has the time to listen.

Defining his role as adviser as analogous to that of "uncle," Wally addresses our fundamental values when he states that "Advisory does not just give us a human face but makes us a caring, compassionate community."

We have many examples of the compassionate community that develops through the deliberate nature of Advisory. Each small group seeks commonality. They connect as human beings by hanging out with each other, playing games, walking to the general store, going out for pizza, arguing, studying, shooting hoops, or sharing mutual boredom. It is a delicate dance.

Athletic director Bill Dod points to our "strong philosophy of caring" as helping his advisees to plan a trip to a local restaurant. His students took the responsibility of teaching a student with very special needs how to behave appropriately in a restaurant.

When faced with the death of a student in his Advisory, Ted Hall recognized the mutual support his group demonstrated. "They made sure that

I did not travel by myself to the cemetery. They made a point of ensuring that I was not the sole caretaker of our group."

We all monitor student academic progress and serve as a liaison for our advisees with their teachers and parents. Beyond that, Advisory is as different as each adviser in the building.

We use what we know. Kierstan Harrow ('98) remembers that Phil Estabrook "brought in cases from his graduate ethics class for us to debate. We also attempted to build a toboggan; we did everything to get the wood ready to steam, and Phil built the steam box. The wood snapped before it was done steaming, so that was sad, but we had such a good time." Brian and Amy McGuigan taught their advisees to merengue and swing dance before the prom. Advisories have also made gingerbread houses together and provided holiday gifts and meals to area charities.

Not every teacher finds comfort daily in Advisory. Some want a daily activity that someone else has designed. According to Alan Gordon, "I believe that comes back to the whole notion that Advisory is not about curriculum, it is about the skill of engaging students in a nonthreatening way." And although we can point to the goals of each grade level in Advisory, its strength is often invisible to the eye. Bill Dod notes that "Advisory is easy to attack because there aren't quantitative ways to measure the value. You can't give a quiz or a test." It is a place, for Nick Rowe, a veteran of more than 25 years in a classroom, to "round out the rough places of my relationships with kids, serving to remind me that they are people, not just students. I need to be reminded that there is more to being a student than rank in class, grades, and scholarship—there is personhood."

Kris Gallo believes:

There shouldn't be school without Advisory. Kids can't fall through the cracks when one adult is in charge of fishing them out of whatever puddle they have just fallen into. I wonder if the tragedy of Columbine would have happened if each of those boys had had an adviser, someone who knew him well?

We honor Advisory's place in our school's life in our graduation ceremonies. Seniors march onto the field with their Advisory, sit together, and receive their diplomas from their adviser, amid many hugs and handshakes.

Whether it serves as triage or celebration, as support or fellowship, Advisory, in Alan Gordon's eyes, is "the most significant way in which we evidence our commitment to personalization. It is the only class that all students take. It is the only class that nearly all our adults teach. Nothing we do here is more student-centered. Nothing we do here is more important."

TEAMS

Our Mission Statement commits us "to support and engage an individual's unique gifts, passions, and interests." By placing our ninth- and tenth-grade students on interdisciplinary teams of approximately 80 students, we have the opportunity to see our students through different lenses. We also grow to see our work from the varying perspectives of our colleagues on team. This interdependent environment encourages us to align our practices with our beliefs. As Peter Senge (1990) says:

> When a team becomes . . . aligned, a commonality of direction emerges, and individuals' energies harmonize. . . . In fact, a resonance or synergy develops, like the "coherent" light of a laser rather than the incoherent and scattered light of a light bulb. There is commonality of purpose, a shared vision, and understanding of how to complement one another's efforts. (p. 234)

When we designed the high school, we recognized that we were transferring students from their existing high school, and we did not want to impact their high school experience with many new structures. Therefore, we kept a traditional structure at grades 11 and 12, Division Two, but in grades 9 and 10, Division One, we established two teams at each grade level. Although the problem of transplanting students would disappear in 3 years, we have kept our Division structures in place; both offer key advantages and disadvantages to students and staff.

During the initial 3 weeks before the opening of Souhegan in September of 1992, Dr. Bob explained to grade-9 and -10 teachers the definition of teams; that is, people who would share common students, a common block of teaching time, and common planning time. And after playing for a long time with creative schedules, we learned that we could not accommodate all voices. Teams would consist of the four disciplines of English, math, science, and social studies, plus a learning specialist, our term for special educators. Teams, two at each of grades 9 and 10, would contain approximately 80 students. Despite our intense growth, we have been able to hold to these student numbers. When teams approached 90 students, we first designed a "miniteam" at grade 9 and 10, asking two teachers to teach two subjects to 40 students. We added a third team to grades 9 and 10 in 1997. Team teachers also serve as academic advisers to 10–12 students, meeting daily in our Advisory Program.

The language of teams is often exclusionary—a teacher is either on-team or off-team. Team time is a continuous block of time that elective teachers must frequently navigate around. When the school needs to create a different schedule to accommodate state testing or special programming, team time is usually preserved at the expense of other courses. Team rooms are usually considered prime real estate in the school; all teams have at least one room with a movable wall to allow for large group activities. Teams design their own narrative progress reports. When conferences about particular students are called for, team teachers meet together as a group with parents; because their meetings are often scheduled during their students' elective periods (common planning time for the team), language teachers and teachers of other elective courses usually cannot attend.

Team teachers teach four periods each day; nonteam teachers often teach an additional course for at least one trimester of the year. Team teachers spend an enormous amount of time together each day, both in class and during common planning time. While the value of this collective time is crucial in support of students' academic, social, and personal needs, it can also lead to what social studies teacher George Darden refers to as "team tunnel vision."

We value teams as a cornerstone concept, but because we do not all function as members of teams, we sometimes resent the time, space, and consideration given to teams of teachers.

Making Teams Work

As math teacher Joann McDeed says, "the good news is we get to make our daily schedule; the bad news is we get to make our daily schedule." The teachers on each of the six teams in Division One (grades 9 and 10) design the time for their 80 or so students, dividing them into four individual classes within a set block of time. The three ninth-grade teams, for instance, meet with their students from 7:30 to 11:15; the tenth-grade teams meet with their students from 9:30 to 11:30 and from 12:15 to 2:10. One team might decide to create a rotating double-block schedule; another team might decide to establish a study period once a week; a third team might use the entire block to work on an interdisciplinary project. One team might establish a very consistent daily schedule, while another team might reconfigure time routinely. Teams, for the most part, have the luxury of allowing the curriculum to drive their schedules.

Teams try to design schedules that make sense for kids. It makes sense to show an entire movie at one sitting, it makes sense for kids to have enough time for their final exhibitions in social studies, and it makes sense to arrange a schedule around a guest speaker. It makes sense to give kids a longer break after an intense performance, and it makes sense to postpone a break if kids haven't completed their work.

Making sense for kids, however, often drives us crazy. Solving for all the variables takes an enormous amount of time, and so team schedules are very fluid. Schedules also take on their own language. Parents seldom understand their child's schedule, but kids learn their schedules no matter how complicated adults make them. Their days make sense to them because they are arranged around the work rather than a rigid master schedule.

The decision to protect the time given to Division One teams has caused conflicts. While this decision creates opportunities for interdisciplinary learning for students on teams, it has the effect of preventing those same opportunities for other courses. Team teachers have common planning times while their students attend elective courses. We recognize that common planning time is essential for strong interdisciplinary curriculum links, but we have not solved the dilemma of providing this time for all the pairings of teachers in our building. Within a 7:30–2:10 schoolday, it is impossible to accommodate all needs for shared time. As a consequence, time, space, and structures have dominated our conversations at Souhegan since the day we opened.

The Interpersonal Side of Teaming

The month of May in a high school means announcements of unexpected resignations and the subsequent shifting of teaching assignments. All schools experience this and cope with it in different ways, but the overlay of team membership complicates the decision making. After we have sorted for gender, experience, similarities, and differences, there is still that amorphous thing—the intangible quality of a good mix of people. Replacing a member of a team is one of our most difficult rites of spring.

We know that teams take time to develop, and we know how difficult it is to change allegiances to a new partner, to develop new habits, new communication strategies, new work. So, is it okay to break up a successful team in order to help to ground a newer, less experienced team? How many new partners should one teacher be expected to work with over a few years? What is the indirect cost of changing partners—does interdisciplinary work fade away with each new pairing, or is there new growth when new partners are grafted together? What happens if the team's goals do not match the goals of the school? What if the performance of either an individual or an entire team is subject to many complaints from parents or colleagues? Should the needs of the institution take precedence over the needs of an established team? How can we equitably resolve all issues raised when one person leaves an established team? The conversations that precede a change of team membership are often difficult, relying heavily on the goodwill of the participants involved in proposed changes. Constant communication, allowing time for change to be contemplated, considering various alternatives, checking assumptions, establishing clear performance standards, avoiding quick fixes, listening hard, respecting individual needs—all are essential components of the group process. There are no shortcuts.

We sometimes think of a square dance as a metaphor for establishing a team. Those in the square bow to their partners, do-si-do to their corners, allemande left, and promenade home, as the caller reconfigures each group to suit the music and the pace.

Joining a team is also somewhat analogous to participating in a Unification Church wedding at which hundreds of brides and grooms exchange vows as they meet each other for the first time. In the case of forming a new team, adults come together to work with 80 or so adolescents, creating many variables joined together in a very intimate setting.

Teams share students, space, tasks, and time; the good of the whole takes precedence over the good of the individual, yet good teams make room for individual needs. Practices and programs have to adjust to the skills of the team.

To be effective, each team must state and affirm core beliefs and establish group norms. Team members must be willing to evaluate the individual and collective performance of the team on a regular basis, to avoid the trap of a group-think mentality. This step is crucial.

While our Mission Statement and the Souhegan Six offer templates for behavioral norms for all members of our learning community, each team must decide how to align itself with these cornerstone concepts. The following snapshots of two tenth-grade teams and the spirited conversations that often arise during common planning time provide a sense of the relationships formed by teams.

Life on Team

Team 10Z. Although the team agreed to talk about life on team, they first needed to discuss some team business. There was some confusion as to when progress reports were due and who had completed their work on the narrative portions. One teacher offered an update on a student who had undergone surgery over the weekend. A schoolwide assembly planned for later in the week necessitated a change in the team's schedule. Kathy Maddock, who is currently job-sharing the team's social studies portion of humanities with Cathy Fischer-Mueller, had a tough time facilitating this conversation, acknowledging that she could not see the big picture. There was a lot of laughter as Kathy tried to spell out all the scheduling options, especially when she announced, "Okay, we're clear on that." The team laughed again when Kathy proclaimed that she might be forced to take over as team captain "because I'm so damn good at it."

With the daily business complete, the team turned its attention to the question of what it means to be on a team:

Cathy Fischer-Mueller, humanities: Our relationship with each other is crucial. The kids see us as adults who like each other, so we are constantly modeling relationships for kids. We take care of each other like families do, in our function and in our dysfunction.

Kris Gallo, math: The struggle of teaming is that when someone is going through something hard, we support that person, but we also feel that pain. Sharing personal or professional challenges with each other creates a vital strength for the team.

Jane Flythe, learning specialist: Team is the best place for someone new to Souhegan to start. Team offers the best teaching practices. I am forced to become a learner because I need to understand the math on team in order to help kids.

Kathy Maddock, humanities: Team allows me to gain an understanding of each kid. Because we pride ourselves on knowing kids well, it is more upsetting on a team when we cannot make a difference to an individual student. When all of us working together can't effect change, it is more upsetting.

Alan Gordon, guidance: Putting heads together with people who know a student from several different perspectives helps that student.

Ann Clifton-Waite, science: There is a sense of security for the kids. They like to identify themselves with a team. In the past couple of years, I needed to lean hard on my teammates while going through a personal hell. We have had some intense conversations that could not happen anyplace else. On a team, we not only get to know who the kids are, we are pretty disrobed. People know you. That's not easy, but it has been very positive.

Aimee Gibbons, humanities: Team is a cohesive unit with different strengths. That makes the unit stronger. For instance, Kris does all of our schedules, except for today when Kathy Maddock tried, and you saw how that worked out!

All of us have our times when we are okay, and not okay, and we all step up when we need to. I had a lot of anxiety about my master's thesis, and my partners encouraged me to take time out of class to get that done. I really appreciated that. They also know that somewhere down the line I will do the same for them. Team is so time-consuming, but without that investment of time, we wouldn't have what team is. It would be lonely and isolating and you wouldn't have any idea of where you were in relation to anybody else.

Brian Irwin, guidance: When I was trying to replicate this type of thing at another high school, I was aware of how often we talk here about kids. In no other forum, in no other place, would that happen. That stems directly from the Mission Statement's call to support and engage each of our students' individual gifts.

Team is so different from other teaching experiences; you are not an independent contractor. I still remember the loneliness of closing your classroom door and walking to the parking lot, the sound of that door closing as you clicked down the hallway. Here, you are not alone. You are a team.

Cathy Fischer-Mueller: With that comes a challenge. Some days I want to be selfish. I want to hear that door shut. It is very hard to hang on to your own agenda and still function on a team.

Kris Gallo: Teams meet, all the time. Mondays, we all meet to discuss our classes for the week and arrange for the best use of Jane's time. On Tuesdays, we discuss kids. Wednesdays, the three tenth-grade teams meet for a double block. Some of those are logistics meetings, but we also present our work to each other, following protocols we learned from our work with the National School Reform Faculty. On Thursdays, we schedule parent meetings, and on Fridays, we have individual time with Jane for modifying curriculum. We also each meet with tenth-grade subject-area teachers once a week. In any given week, we have no time to ourselves. None. Team planning can take all the time.

Ann Clifton-Waite: Officially, I should have maybe 3 to 4 hours each week available to me on paper, but it doesn't seem to happen. I am, however, really excited about my work this year. We have a new learning specialist on our team, and I am working with her almost every day. She provides this other voice that helps me plan for all students.

Kris Gallo: You pay a very heavy cost, but I am willing to pay that cost to be on a team. Teams allow students to be known by a group of teachers who work together every day with the same groups of students.

Kathy Maddock: One of the very best moments for me on team was last year when I told my team I was pregnant. They went nuts—that really epitomizes the positive aspects of team.

Team 10Y. Although Team 10Z has been together for a few years, the members of one of the other tenth-grade teams, 10Y, are new to each other this year. Gavin Sturges, who teaches English, is new to the school, a transplant from Great Britain. Math teacher Lee Gast is a second-year teacher who worked with another team last year. Phil Estabrook came to Souhegan as a tenth-grade social studies intern and worked on a ninth-grade team for 3 years. Jenny Deenik also began working at Souhegan as an intern and is now in her fourth year of teaching science. This team defied all the laws of probability—all four teachers welcomed new babies within 2 months of each other during the current school year. Sally Houghton, the team's learning specialist, is a charter member of the Souhegan faculty.

Phil Estabrook, social studies: In order for a team to function well, the chemistry is crucial. Everything we do is valuable, but I wish I had more time. I feel pulled a lot. Sometimes I want to pull myself somewhere.

Gavin Sturges, English: I do not view meeting time as a loss of personal time. It is not a particular tension for me.

Jenny Deenik, science: One benefit of spending so much time with each other is that curriculum ideas sometimes just happen. My work on inventions happened through listening to my humanities partners discuss their unit on the labor movement. It occurred to me that I could ask students to explore inventions that changed the way humans used energy. Suddenly, we had connections to the Civil War with the development of the cotton gin. We saw that the development of the sewing machine opened up completely new industries in urban areas. My work was spontaneous—it did not come as part of an extensive plan.

Lee Gast, math: Last year, team kept me sane. I was a first-year teacher, I had moved and lost a box of stuff, and my wife and I were living with relatives. Basically, I survived my first year.

Sally Houghton, learning specialist: This is my eighth year on a team; I have worked with a wide variety of teachers. As an experienced team member, I am an effective facilitator of meetings with parents of special-needs students. Particularly on a new team, my expertise in these areas is a benefit to the team.

Scott Prescott, a math teacher on Team 10X, points to another advantage of life on team. He became aware during a faculty meeting of some widespread dissatisfaction with a recent administrative decision. Scott believes that the collegiality on team diminishes a lot of tension that individual teachers might feel. He says:

Teams provide a filter for initial impressions of most issues. We don't sit around and talk about school issues. We talk about our students and about our work. We laugh, we get mad, we move on. One of us might notice that we are all grouchy, but we name the feeling, laugh, and move on. I feel an active sense of collegiality and support.

Good teams work hard to maximize their potential. They are aware of the curriculum and assessment strategies of their teammates. They look for connections between their disciplines. They talk about ways to be more effective with individual students. They form a sense of family, with particular habits, traditions, and expectations. Team membership offers as much to the adults as it does to the students they teach. Team teachers frequently list as strengths of working on a team the fact that they are known well by a group of supportive peers, that they receive support and security, that being part of a group develops consistency and offers a sense of belonging.

Teachers who begin working on teams usually choose to stay on teams. Occasionally, a teacher will express an interest in teaching a course not offered on team, or in working with older students, and we try to accommodate those desires. Teachers initially hired to teach in Division Two, however, do not generally request a move to Division One. Teachers who do not work on teams cite the investment of time required as the primary reason for not choosing to serve on a team.

We have had conversations about defining teams differently, perhaps linking language to a team, or eliminating math from team, or blending different academic disciplines onto teams, but we have not yet altered our basic team structure. Foreign-language teachers, art teachers, and teachers from other disciplines teach across the 4 years of school; limiting their work to one grade level would cause a substantial increase to our personnel budget and would cause complex scheduling problems.

Teaming and Collaboration

> If teams learn, they become a microcosm for learning throughout the organization. Insights gained are put into action. . . . The team's accomplishments can set the tone and establish a standard for learning together for the larger organization. (Senge, 1990, p. 236)

Common planning time and common groups of students plus the camaraderie of group members who know each other's strengths and needs lead to connections between academic disciplines. We can cite many examples of informal, timely curricular connections, but the true benefit of a cohesive team is the opportunity to provide students with a different way of knowing. Joann McDeed discusses the work of one ninth-grade team in providing curriculum connections for students.

> Knowing that we would introduce an interdisciplinary unit in April allowed us to incorporate the necessary skill building in our work

throughout the year. It is easy to document student learning in this unit. What is fascinating to me is that so much of our work with students is mirrored in our work with each other. Teams are so intimate in nature. When we work closely together, it becomes clear that adults also have very different learning styles and are a real heterogeneous mix. It is very frustrating to have a meeting where you have to repeat information to some individuals because they missed an important meeting. Sometimes team members do not meet deadlines and tempers flare. It happens; you move on. Actually, that's not quite accurate. Sometimes our differences clearly spilled over into other areas of our work as a team. Once we had to call a time-out and lay out all our frustrations so that we could continue to work together.

Developing authentic curriculum and assessment requires mutual respect and trust on the part of the adults working together. Joann underscores the need for teachers to work on the same skills we ask our students to develop in a collegial, collaborative environment. There are no shortcuts to group process. Relationships are much messier than textbooks, but we have learned that if we give people time to work together, they choose to work together, and their collaboration improves student learning and raises the standard of expectations.

We have also learned that it is difficult to replicate curriculum that has been developed as part of one individual's or one team's passion for the work. We all work on building student skills, but we often make individual choices in how to work on those skills—what ideas, practices, or approaches we will bring to bear.

One example of team collaboration is the ninth-grade rocket launch; our 270 ninth-grade students start their year building rockets in their science and math class. Science teacher Vince Tom says:

> One of the essential aspects of the success of this unit is the ability to adjust time. Block schedules allow for time to think, question, and do. The opportunity to work with my teammates to reconfigure time and space to meet the curricular needs of my students makes this work possible. The opportunity for my teammates to see students work in a different academic discipline helps all of us in our work with kids. When I share my project sheets and rubrics with my peers on my team, I share my expectations for student engagement.
>
> The only thing that makes it possible to accomplish this level of integration of curriculum is the flexible schedules of the ninth-grade teams. Without common planning time, this work is impossible.

Students leave the Division One team structure at the end of grade 10, and enter Division Two (grades 11 and 12). We have not been able to ensure common planning time in all cases to teachers who do pair their courses in Division Two; consequently, they have a harder time consistently linking their curriculum across disciplines. It is ironic that although we understand totally the benefits that accrue from providing teams of teachers with common planning times, we have not found a way to meet all needs within the construct of a typical school day.

AN INCLUSIVE COMMUNITY

An inclusive community is manifest with democracy—we all have a voice and are treated equally; we can transcend all labels. Democracy means inclusion of all sorts—intellectual, economic, social, racial, ethnic. At Souhegan, the desire to serve as a democratic community mandates a culture that honors differences in individuals. Those differences are seen as assets, not stigmas. By acknowledging differences, we encourage all members to share their individuality and to know that in that sharing they will be safe.

An old cartoon shows a teacher looking at her class, each of whom wears a label—anorexic, dyslexic, math whiz, asthmatic, pregnant, gifted, alcoholic, athlete, and so forth. There is truth to the picture in that our classes are filled with individuals with complex definitions and abilities, but those differences do not serve to label or exclude. Depending on the task, we as teachers also bring varying gifts to the table, gifted perhaps on one task, average or learning disabled on another. When communicating a team's progress report for a given student, one teacher excels; she enjoys public speaking and does a good job at addressing parents at public forums. When working on the team's rocket project, however, she is lost. She needs far more help than she offers. The teachers on this team are as heterogeneous as the students; their abilities and skills shift according to the task at hand.

In viewing ourselves in this way, we remain more sensitive to the heterogeneous needs of our students. Consequently, we do not sort our students according to ability in our classrooms because their abilities vary according to task. It makes more sense to vary the task than to "track" the student.

Comments About Heterogeneous Grouping

Parents frequently pose two arguments against heterogeneous grouping. The first argument blames the high school for not providing the motivation to students who are not eager to succeed in their studies. That is a difficult argument because those students lacking in motivation in school also exhibit that same behavior at home. If it is frustrating to the parents of that child at home, it is more frustrating to teach that child in a setting with 20 or more other children. We could resort to requiring students to complete mimeographed worksheets, thereby ensuring that they will be busy, but busy does not equal mastery or progress toward stated learning goals.

The other argument regarding heterogeneity states that this type of environment holds back the academically gifted students. Research has proven otherwise. We asked several graduates from Souhegan's class of 1998 to discuss, in light of their subsequent college experiences, their participation in heterogeneous classes.

Gayle Willis (Georgia Tech) spoke about the development of leadership skills in a heterogeneous environment.

> I learned to make my work accessible to others, to work in a group. Motivating other people is a necessary skill in life. I will be successful if I can help others to love what they are doing and help everybody to recognize their contribution to the process and the product.

The group laughed when Holly Mauro (New York University) proclaimed her love of learning.

> I know that Souhegan gave me learning processes, but I felt like I was in chains during high school. I am glad that I learned skills, but I wish I had learned them in a different context. I do not appreciate heterogeneity. I am not a patient person; I don't want to be with people who do not care about their learning. I want to excel, and I want to be with people who want to excel. I love the Stern School at NYU.

For Kerry Silva (Brown University), the success of heterogeneity depends on strong motivation.

> When everyone in a group works well towards a common goal, mixed ability groups can produce great results. Some of my best projects in ninth and tenth grade were with people who wanted to do great work; we all brought different strengths. I believe in heterogeneous grouping in an ideal sense, but, honestly, my experience with grouping depended on the motivation, not necessarily the abilities, of the individuals.

Elizabeth Lenaghan (Tufts University) believes that the Souhegan philosophy is a great motivator.

> I was so willing to buy into the entire Souhegan philosophy. In ninth grade, I did projects with people I had never worked with before, people I would never have chosen to work with. I worked hard to motivate others. Over time, the idealism starts to dissolve, but when people buy into the philosophy, they work harder.

Laura Emond (Bowdoin College) agrees with her classmates on motivation serving as a key learning tool. She says, "The benefit of Souhegan was that there was no stratification between teachers and students. I thought of my high school teachers as a resource, individuals who were in tune with their students and with their own learning."

Matt Sullivan (Rensselaer Polytechnical Institute) says, "At Souhegan, I knew deeply that respect between teachers and students was an important value. I was shocked to learn that one of my college professors didn't have a personal interest in the performance of his students."

Josh Deslisle (University of New Hampshire) nodded as Matt spoke of the respect he felt during high school. "I was psyched to be at the high school. My freshman teachers did a great job of making the school mine. I bought into the whole philosophy and felt a great deal of mutual respect."

Gayle Willis believes that she has an advantage over other students at Georgia Tech in terms of approaching professors for help: "Souhegan taught me that my teachers are my peers because everybody is still learning."

These students identified motivation rather than innate ability as a key to a successful classroom experience for a particular assignment or subject. Their conversation also reveals the value of a respectful learning environment as well as strong relationships with teachers as key motivators for all students. Clearly, these factors transcend issues of student grouping, which have become a preoccupation with both educators and parents.

Our Barometers

We have many barometers of success—students who succeed because they have always achieved, and students with serious challenges who have succeeded for the first time, both academically and socially. We like to tell the story of a nonverbal student in an English class who could only say "yes" and "no." During a poetry workshop, the students in his work group, recognizing his language limitations, wrote a poem with a refrain that required the use of these two words. He cheerfully exchanged "high-fives" with his group at the end of this reading. This student's skills grew far more than we had anticipated; his classmates learned, too. They never marginalized this student, including him routinely in classroom and social experiences.

Jimmy was an extremely troubled child. He threw books and furniture in anger in the classroom. He was afraid whenever anyone stood behind him, and seldom made eye contact, hiding behind the brim of his ever-present black hat. His teachers spoke to his peers, stating that in order for everyone to feel safe in school, each individual needed to feel safe, and that this student interpreted information differently from others. He could not "read" situations well, often bolting out of class when he felt threatened. When that happened, a teacher would follow him to his hiding place beneath the gym bleachers and wait quietly until he was ready to return. His classmates learned to continue their work if the teacher had to leave for a few minutes, demonstrating their understanding of and their respect for individual safety. Over time, this student began to trust others, ever so slowly, and became a participant in the classroom environment. By his senior year, his black hat was long gone, he smiled easily, and he had made a group of friends. He completed his course requirements and his Senior Project, and he graduated from Souhegan. In his final reflection, he noted that this place was "different" and that he had been accepted.

As is true in every school, we also have a group of students that we have not helped, kids who, despite the goodwill and good work of a large number of adults, cannot learn either in our setting or "on our clock." We can adjust our setting, adjust to the identified needs of their education plans, but we cannot ensure success for every child. There are sometimes too many variables at play. And, although intellectually we understand that some kids cannot learn on our timetable, we also have trouble accepting that even one child cannot learn here. We know that every child, even the most severely challenged, has at least one adult advocate, but that is sometimes not enough. Eric Mann, our coordinator of special services, calls these students "the tweeners." They don't slip between the cracks—we have too many supports in place—but they stand in that liminal space between home and school, between childhood and adolescence, between adolescence and adulthood, between success and failure. Trying to find a way to make a substantive difference to these students is, according to one faculty member, like nailing Jell-O to the wall.

Perspectives from Two Special Services Directors

We do not carry these children alone. We have the benefit of working with strong advocates for inclusion who help us to find tools to bridge the gap between our ideals and the tension of daily reality.

Kathy Skoglund, director of special services for the school districts of Amherst and Mont Vernon, offers a historical perspective of our path toward full inclusion and the challenges it presents for all of us. Eric Mann, coordinator of special services at Souhegan High School, confronts both the universal and particular frustrations of an environment of inclusion. Eric also discusses the factors leading to excellent teaching in an inclusive environment and the times when inclusion fails students.

Kathy Skoglund. Traditionally, 15 or 20 years ago, students with special education needs were, almost without exception, segregated and isolated because it was believed that they required unique kinds of instruction that other kinds of children didn't need, and that the presence of those children with special needs would be disruptive or would take away from the educational experience of the others. It occurred to those working in special education that there would be benefits for all children if we brought them together, so we started in tiny ways to do just that.

We began to include students from self-contained classrooms in activities in the regular education classrooms whenever appropriate. What became evident was that the kids with special needs were extremely good at watching and imitating positive behavior they saw in the regular education classroom. They also modeled inappropriate behavior, but the results were far more positive than negative. The initial thrust was around socialization and developing social skills. As we worked on that and expanded into different areas of curriculum, we also became aware that these children were developing cognitive skills and intellectual knowledge that we had not expected. That then became our incentive to continue and accelerate our work.

We had so many possibilities to tap into, but we knew we had to do a lot of work in the area of teacher support, materials, timelines, and assessment. We also had to prepare students to be in a classroom. We were introducing students who had very particular disabilities, who had never been in a regular classroom. We had to help everyone understand that these students learned differently and they spoke differently and they needed to be assessed differently. Parent education, student education, teacher education—all were integral aspects of this work. We had to prove, across the board, that we knew what we were doing, that we would see changes in these children, cognitively and socially.

We made the deliberate decision to open Souhegan as a school of full inclusion after many years of experience with inclusion at the elementary level. Much groundwork has to go into this work. There are no shortcuts, no immediate fixes. In existing settings, it simply doesn't work to mandate this change, to suddenly announce that a school will incorporate, today, all students into one setting. What made it possible at Souhegan was that we were stating our beliefs and our intended practices very publicly before the school opened. All applicants for positions knew that their classes would contain a wide variety of students with a wide variety of needs. We did not have to change existing practices; we had to establish our mindset and provide appropriate levels of support.

One particular concern is that higher education has not begun to address the need to prepare teachers to work with students with special needs. In order to obtain a teaching degree, or a certificate to teach, individuals have to take one or two courses in special education, but it is not part of the university culture to teach future teachers about how to deal with a multilevel classroom. This is wrong. American classrooms have children with widely varying abilities and interest levels and backgrounds and readiness for learning, regardless of whether a particular classroom has a child with Down syndrome or autism or severe learning disabilities. This reality mandates a strong need for ongoing professional development. Teachers need consistent help.

There are many ways to document the success of inclusion. In the case of one student, a young man with severe autism, we observe that his peers accept his presence. They understand his disability, and so his behaviors are not the subject of derision; by the same token, he is learning to mitigate his behaviors as he becomes more comfortable with his external environment. There is a genuine reciprocity of learning when we do not hide uncomfortable topics from our students. And the best benefit is the growth in tolerance and acceptance of all sorts of differences.

A prime example of that is observing the behavior of a peer group. We have already noted the success of one particular nonverbal student whose diagnosis remains elusive. We learned that he could learn to a much greater extent than we first thought possible. He was very popular with his classmates, who included him in both learning and social activities. He was crowned King of the Prom. His friends, determined to ensure that he experienced every aspect of high school, even helped him cut class once. He served detention for his behavior, the same disciplinary action as for any other student.

We have had students enmeshed in the environment and others who have had a more peripheral high school experience. The difference is the student's approachability, his or her ability to engage another individual. If there is some exchange, verbal or nonverbal, there will be a much higher degree of socialization. The more we include students of all abilities and disabilities in a common setting, and the earlier we include all students, the more engagement we will develop. We become desensitized to the disability and more attuned with the human connection.

The subject of socialization in a high school setting is complex. There is a body of thought that the adult community must make social inclusion happen, that adults should fix all social wrongs. We know, however, that in an adolescent population, there is an element that we cannot control. We can make students go through the motions, but we cannot make them engage. We can establish norms within our classrooms that all students will be included, and we can even arrange for students to sit together in the cafeteria. We cannot, however, orchestrate the inclusion of particular students in phone calls after school, or parties or get-togethers. We cannot legislate friendship. And we can't do that for any student, let alone those with very special physical, behavioral, intellectual, or emotional challenges.

If we start with an assumption of equality very early in our children's lives, though, we can make a difference, and that difference will remain constant throughout. To accomplish this, we need the active participation of all parents and all teachers.

Inclusion of all students is a core belief, but this belief needs periodic affirmation by all practitioners. Once affirmed, it needs consistent, active support. We have not put enough of our resources into our beliefs. If we truly believe that all students can reach their potential in our classrooms, then we must support the resources to help all students in our multilevel classrooms—students with incredible insights and abilities, those with strong metacognitive skills, the middle-of-the-road gang, and those with learning disabilities.

We need stronger links between schools in our district. We need to ask, "What happened in the grade this child came from?" and "What needs to happen in the grade he goes to next?" We can learn from each other. Our history shows us that progress always begins with a few people willing to talk about their work, and others willing to ask questions that lead to a change in practice. Without this sustained focus, we address situations in too much of a piecemeal fashion.

We definitely have a needier population than we had 10 years ago. Family systems have changed, health systems have changed, the very air we breathe has affected the number of asthma cases our pediatricians address every day. In the area of special education, we have syndromes now that we did not know about 10 years ago, such as Asperger syndrome or pervasive developmental disorder, and now we have multiple students with these syndromes in our schools. The layers of challenges we face are very deep. We cannot make all kids ready at the same time. They do not all learn to read at the same time; they do not all master complex math skills at the same time or in the same context. I cannot imagine a more difficult job than teaching in a classroom.

Eric Mann. Souhegan High School was given a great gift and opportunity, one not afforded most American high schools; Souhegan was created. It was not re-created, re-formed, evolved, or transformed. It began as a concept and was created through the diligence of its founding group of educators. This fact should not be lost upon those who observe this school amid the boundless energy of its youth. Born to nurturing and attentive caregivers, Souhegan has been raised in the functional light of optimism, democracy, respect, and praise. At Souhegan, thinking is encouraged, growth is demanded, and learning is for all members of the community. At Souhegan, teachers view "inclusion" through the eyes of learners: open, curious, thoughtful. It is only in such a learning community that inclusion, mandated by our government but not yet accepted or understood by the masses, can function effectively.

Effective inclusion cannot be mandated. Despite this reality, across America various models of inclusive education are being mandated by superintendents and principals in response to the congressional directive that students must be educated in the general education environment to the maximum extent possible. Force-feeding a concept that is so dependent on the commitment of the whole system and so reliant on those who are providing direct services to students truly begs the dysfunction that often follows. Successful inclusion has its finest opportunity when everyone involved in the system—including school board members, principal, educators, paraprofessionals, custodians, secretarial staff, cafeteria workers, students, and parents of students—commits to and invests in what is essentially a societal commitment, one that values respect, diversity, belonging, and the importance and contribution of each member of the system.

The commitment cannot be exclusively theoretical. It must be backed with resources that intelligently and comprehensively support the system. Effective inclusion does not work without excellence in educators. Effective inclusion does not exist without assurance of adequate numbers of capable support staff to meet the vast learning needs of a diverse student population. If these elements are not in place, the effective practice of inclusive education is elusive.

Student failure in schools that have not effectively supported inclusion results in a myriad of pervasive systemic feelings. These feelings grow from disappointment, doubt, feelings of inadequacy, and frustration. Left unprocessed, the system leads individuals to the comfort of isolation, avoidance, and denial. These systemic responses are the antithesis of the systemic response to effective inclusion. Effective inclusion inspires energy, flexibility, growth, and optimism. Souhegan has, to date, avoided many of the pitfalls of inclusion gone awry, but it still fails to meet the needs of all students.

Inclusion begins through creation of systemic factors that foster feelings of normality and belonging. When the student enters the classroom, he should anticipate that his learning needs will be understood and honored. There must be, in any educational setting, the recognition that students enter the classroom in various stages of development and are transitioning from a variety of environments and circumstances. They have differences in their physical, cognitive, emotional, and social development. They have diversity in their ability to tolerate frustration and to control their impulses. They vary in attention, focus, and distractibility. And they differ in what interests and motivates them. The ability to cope with frustration, challenge, and the extraordinary range of human emotion that affects access to education is different for each individual in the classroom. The effective teacher in an inclusive classroom must be highly attuned to the individuals in the classroom and be prepared to respond to the developmental challenges of each student. For teachers to address all the developmental needs in their classrooms every day would be impossible; to ignore, or not attempt to address these needs, violates the commitment to respect and honor each learner.

An inclusive school that also values recognizing and honoring of individual needs must also be able and willing to recognize when the intensity or particular circumstances relating to an individual's challenges requires more than the school can provide. Pragmatism should always be considered ahead of the philosophical commitment to inclusion. When inclusion is not working for a student, the healthy system must do collectively what we ask students and faculty to do individually—self-observe and reflect honestly and critically. Well-functioning inclusive systems are self-assured in their values but are never characterized by an arrogance that promotes reluctance to view their scars and limitations.

Educators who are effective in inclusive classrooms share common attributes: the ability to establish mutually respectful rapport with students; the ability to establish an aura of leadership or authority, while simultaneously encouraging a democratic and open classroom system; the ability and willingness to reflect and to be aware of the impact of feelings/emotions on behavioral choices; the ability to think creatively and with flexibility about how to reach students. Excellent teachers also tend to be open to sharing and collaborating with other professionals and paraprofessionals, are aware of boundaries with students and parents, are attuned to the development of the emotional and social lives of students, are willing and able to expend time and energy planning lessons that reach all students, and are willing and able to seek direction and support when they are unsure—all this in addition to intelligence, a bright and positive personality, emotional stability, confidence, a strong foundation in subject area, a good sense of humor, a dash of dynamism, and a genuine enjoyment of being with children.

Given this elaborate description of an excellent inclusion educator, it is not difficult to see that staffing an entire school is an enormous challenge. Additionally, maintaining the quality throughout years of growth and change is a formidable task. Promoting optimism and hopefulness, while providing support, encouragement, and training, helps to keep the system from the cynicism and apathy that eat away at the fabric of so many public schools.

The existence of teams in ninth and tenth grade helps to keep the system open, reflective, and accountable. These teams include a team member who is specifically trained in special needs. In teams that function optimally, there is a clear recognition by all team members that all educators are teachers of special-needs students. There is not the "my student/your student" mentality that pervades so many schools when viewing teaching responsibilities for disabled and nondisabled students. Learning specialists at Souhegan are viewed by students as available to all students, and they attempt to provide input about teaching techniques that will benefit all students. Student learning and behavioral issues are approached collectively and supportively.

When does full inclusion fail students? The concept of "full inclusion," whereby educators are expected to educate students with a wide range of learning differences and abilities within a classroom, is extremely challenging and, as previously stated, requires excellence in teaching as well as thoughtful planning. A commitment to full inclusion and heterogeneous education by its nature does not allow for traditional special education models such as tracked education (levels of difficulty), special education replacement classrooms (slower-paced, modified curriculum; class sizes of six to eight learning-disabled students), or resource rooms (classrooms designed for varying degrees of academic support for special-needs students). The downside of these special education models is that students in the lower-level or special education classes are grouped with students of like ability; often these classes are not challenging to many of the students. These classes tend to include not only students who academically cannot manage the high language requirements of the mainstream but also underachieving, undermotivated students who often exhibit immature behaviors and low self-esteem with respect to academics. Thus, the culture within these classes tends to be one of minimal expectations and low levels of energy in academic pursuit.

This is not to say that students with learning disabilities (LD) should be stereotyped as low achievers. To the contrary, many LD students achieve despite their challenges. Full inclusion assures that no student with learning disabilities will be thrown into an unchallenging, unmotivating learning environment. The downfall of full inclusion, interestingly, is that there are indeed no classes to turn to when the curriculum is too challenging, or the educators have not adequately planned, or the teachers are simply not able to understand the student's learning challenge. When these inevitable circumstances occur, students fail, and the search begins for alternative ways to assist the student.

Souhegan has needed to implement supports for students that tend to belie the concept of full inclusion. Academic support, paraprofessional support, and individualized supports provided by reading specialists, academic tutors, speech and language pathologists, and counselors have helped students with disabilities. These supports provide both academic and emotional support for students on a daily basis within the context of a fully inclusive program. A number of students have required the structure of behavioral contracts to provide the external structure required for them to succeed. When Souhegan is unable to meet the learning or behavior-management needs of students, full-time alternative placements are sought.

As Souhegan has grown, so has the need to provide individualized support for students. As these supports grow in number and in cost, the temptation to revert to traditional special education increases. As Kathy Skoglund has noted, there are few educators with experience in this type of education and there are many who have received little or no training. The need for individualized attention complicates the process of planning. With less time to plan with learning specialists, classroom teachers have less input on how the goals and expected outcomes of lessons can be attained by all learners.

The truth is that many teachers struggle with teaching all learners and that the opportunity for every teacher to plan with learning specialists is sporadic. While the energy is abundant at Souhegan, and the commitment to personalization is powerful, even Souhegan falls short in its ability to effectively reach all learners. Full inclusion, to Souhegan's credit, does not give the option of special education classrooms, but as a result, the school finds itself in a quandary about the growth of necessary individualized supports.

CHAPTER 4

Beyond Seat Time

Most of the work in the emerging economy requires an ability to learn on the job, to discover what needs to be known and to find and use it quickly. Many of the new jobs depend on creativity—an out-of-the-box thinking, originality and flair. Almost by definition, standardized tests can't measure these sorts of things. They're best at measuring the ability to regurgitate facts and apply standard modes of analysis. (Reich, 2001, p. 48)

At the heart of our work at Souhegan lie two major student exhibitions—the Division One Exhibition and the Senior Project. Each serves as a culminating rite of passage; and each represents the core of our belief system about teaching and learning, namely, that students should be engaged in an authentic task, should be given clear expectations and accompanying rubrics, should be asked to focus on process as well as substance, should take the primary initiative in bringing a substantial piece of work to fruition, should be expected to present themselves both orally and in writing, and should be called upon to do significant reflection upon the work accomplished.

Both efforts represent significant undertakings for students. Both expect teachers to commit themselves "beyond the call of duty." Over our short history as a school, both have also transcended their functions as student assessment tools. They have been embraced by the Amherst/Mont Vernon communities as collective events that manifest the finest examples of Souhegan's mission and practice.

This chapter creates a context for the philosophy and development of both forms of exhibition and then provides descriptions and reflections about the two programs as they have evolved over 9 years.

In the current climate of high-stakes testing in our schools, it is important to recognize that these tests, most often standardized in nature, are only useful as indicators of some small part of a student's acquired knowledge base, at best a demonstration of competency in a few discrete areas of information. Beyond that, the Carnegie units required by most American high schools measure the completion of traditional standards of coursework—so many units of English, math, and so on.

We believe that schools must hold students accountable for a higher set of standards than those addressed by state assessments or by typical coursework. In our view, students must be required to demonstrate such skills as complex thinking, problem solving, self-management, collaboration, and reflection. As Matt Irwin ('03) noted when he transferred to Souhegan, "Other schools ask students to do; Souhegan asks kids to think about what they do."

Our standards establish what we want all students to know and be able to do, beyond the acquisition of knowledge. To that end, our graduation requirements include 4 years of participation in our daily Advisory Program, successful completion of the Division One Exhibition at the end of tenth grade, a research paper in eleventh grade, an intensive Senior Project, and 40 hours of comunity service. In addition, we require the students to meet learning expectations in academic and nonacademic courses at a basic proficiency level (not less than a grade of C-). As noted earlier, our standards apply to *all* students. Moreover, we open our standards to public scrutiny by inviting parents and residents of Amherst and Mont Vernon to attend our Division One Exhibition and our Senior Project presentations.

Emphasis on state testing has diverted national attention from the need to require students to think and to develop deep understanding of substantive issues. For example, by modeling democratic practices in our classrooms and in our school governance, we require our students to demonstrate civic responsibility and to show us evidence of their status as active citizens in a democratic society.

Souhegan High School offers students two major opportunities to demonstrate their work to the larger learning community. At the end of tenth grade, all students present 2 years' worth of portfolio work, and their reflections on that work, to a roundtable of parents, teachers, and peers. They engage in a deep, substantive, and usually powerful conversation about their progress, their strengths, and their challenges. They present a portfolio of work that documents their progress toward Souhegan's learner expectations. Collectively, they offer a wealth of data about our work with students.

The Division One Exhibition celebrates student achievement. The public nature of the Exhibition also serves to caulk whatever cracks exist for students who will require additional support as they leave the team environment for the second half of their high school years. As we examine their portfolios, we can help them map out a plan to address shortcomings that exist in their skill development.

Every Souhegan student must also complete a Senior Project, a serious independent study requiring active research and application. It provides the opportunity for synthesis of all the skills of academic scholarship acquired over 12 years of study in different disciplines. Again, the public display of those skills documents for the community the values instilled in their students and their readiness for whatever challenges their futures hold. By asking students to invest in their learning beyond serving seat time, we attend to both their minds and their hearts.

THE DIVISION ONE EXHIBITION

Educators have always believed that schools have the power to change lives. At Souhegan, we believe, as Deborah Meier (2000) has stated, that

> The kinds of learning required by citizens cannot be accomplished by standardized and centrally imposed systems of learning. . . . Human learning, to be efficient, effective, and long-lasting, requires the engagement of learners, on their own behalf, and rests on the relationships between schools and their communities, between teachers and their students, and between the individual learner and what is to be learned. (p. 18)

At Souhegan, we have done much to accommodate the building of those relationships, but in our third year of operation, we recognized that we wanted to formalize those relationships, to mark them in some way. What we were seeking was an academic Bar Mitzvah, a true rite of passage for students as they left the structured Division One team experience and entered Division Two for their last 2 years of high school. We wanted to build on the relationships that students had developed with their teachers, to ask the powerful grown-ups in our students' lives to hold up a mirror for students to peer deeply into themselves, to acknowledge their gifts and skills, and to reflect on both academic strengths and weaknesses. We wanted them to tell us who they were, what they believed, what knowledge they had acquired, what they still had to learn. We wanted them to have that experience while they still had the luxury of time to change and to grow. We also wanted to ensure that our tenth-grade students were prepared for the work they would encounter during their last 2 years of high school in our Division Two. Thus the Division One Exhibition became as much an accountability measure of our success as a school as it was a test of our students. We were interested in learning the answers to four main questions:

- How do we improve student performance?
- How do we gauge the improvement of student performance?
- How do we provide meaningful information on student performance to students, parents, and other institutions?
- What do we want students to know and be able to do when they leave Division One?

Tom Pado and Cathy Fischer-Mueller, tenth-grade humanities teachers, took the lead in helping the faculty through a series of complex conversations and structured protocols to design a way to document student performance during the first 2 years of high school. Tom recognized that:

We needed to know how to design and use authentic, credible, and effective forms of assessing student work, and we realized that until we could provide useful and timely feedback, student performance would never improve. We also recognized that we needed to agree on specific standards in order to hold both students and teachers accountable for quality student work. While determining these standards of performance, we were conscious of the fact that we needed to allow a diverse group of students with a variety of intelligences to achieve these standards in different ways.

Getting this far took a lot of effort and time. Every conversation led us in slightly different directions as we struggled to figure out how to design an assessment tool that would allow us and our students to recognize their successes and their struggles.

On the way home from visiting roundtable exhibitions at University Heights High School in the Bronx, Tom and Cathy reviewed everything they had learned about documenting student work from conversations with teachers at Lindbloom High School in Chicago, Central Park East High School, and University Heights High School. Cathy remembers:

During that 4-hour car ride in 100-degree weather with no air conditioner, we recognized that although we could incorporate many elements from each school we had studied, we could not adopt an off-the-shelf model for our work with our students. We had to create our own. We had traveled a long way to realize that our answer of how to organize our Division One Exhibition had its roots in the assessment model we already used at Souhegan. Students were familiar with our Learner Expectations; we would ask students to use examples from each of their courses to document their progress toward becoming:

- Knowledgeable persons
- Complex thinkers
- Effective communicators
- Self-directed learners
- Skilled information processors
- Collaborative workers
- Responsible citizens

We would ask students to demonstrate to their parents, their teachers, their peers, and their communities the habits and skills and knowledge that we most value.

Tenth-grade students already participated in two forms of standardized assessments, the New Hampshire State Assessments and the PSATs. We recognize what these tests can and cannot measure. As Tom Pado says:

> Standardized testing is limited when gathering evidence of a student's ability to use and apply knowledge in the context of real-life problem solving. Tests do not fully measure the knowledge and skills that learning communities value and often attempt to assess knowledge that communities do not value.

Our students routinely participate in performance-based assessments. The Division One Exhibition gives us the opportunity to generate information about what students know and are able to do as a result of 2 years of work in our classrooms.

What Is the Division One Exhibition?

The Division One Exhibition process consists of four phases: collection, selection, reflection, and connection. During their ninth- and tenth-grade years, students collect their work in all courses and place them in working folders, maintained by classroom teachers in each discipline.

Tenth grade advisers help students to select work and place it in their Division One Exhibition binder. This is a very active stage in the learning process. Advisers ask their advisees to talk about why the work matters, what the student did well, what is missing from the work. Advisers ask their students to think about what the work reveals about their commitment to their studies. Advisers use their own meeting time to calibrate the conversations they are having with their students and to monitor the overall progress of the work.

By the end of tenth grade, all students have a collection of work that represents progress in each of the Souhegan Learner Expectations. Students select a wide range of assignments for their portfolios. Sometimes they choose an assignment that demonstrates their best effort, but they are just as likely to include a range of tests, essays, papers, visuals, and so forth that demonstrate growth over time.

Students reflect on each piece of work they select. In addition, students write a detailed letter to their roundtable. The intent of this letter is to provide students with the opportunity to reflect on their experiences in relation to Souhegan's Mission Statement and to provide the reader with a clear picture of the student as learner. The letter is structured so that students can make connections between their past learning experiences and the present.

Finally, students engage in a structured reflective conversation on their experiences. Each student engages in a 45-minute dialogue about his or her work with a roundtable consisting of peers/advocates, teachers, and parents and/or community members. These roundtables take place during 3 days of exam periods in June. Tenth-grade advisers attend the roundtables of their 10 advisees; every other Souhegan teacher and guidance counselor participates in at least one roundtable.

Students are expected to engage in serious and respectful dialogue about their work with roundtable participants. They are also expected to address inquiries from guests and to respond to feedback that shows learning and growth. Students are expected to make connections between their Division One work, Souhegan's Mission Statement and their past, present, and future experiences. We have developed a fairly strict protocol for the roundtables to bring consistency and to ensure that every student has the opportunity to meet these high expectations.

Cathy Fischer-Mueller notes that the fact that tenth-grade team teachers meet each week to develop curriculum, plan grade-level activities, and resolve discipline issues greatly affected the design and execution of this initiative. After meeting for several weeks in small groups to design the rubric, Cathy noted:

> The consistency of our philosophy produced remarkably similar work. We had a history together; we trusted each other. Even so, we were stunned when we realized we had nailed it! It was a magic moment—we had huge smiles as we gave each other high-fives. We knew we were creating something extremely special for our students. The rubric underscored our Mission Statement and focused on reflection, on making connections, on providing evidence of thoughtful learning.
>
> We had been working on this process for several months; by February 1996, we knew we had to present it to our students. We

had talked about launching it the first year with a sample group of 20 kids or so. Then we decided to just do it—the "Ready, Fire, Aim" approach. We had a deep sense that our design was inherently good, but we knew we could not improve it until we worked on it with students. We told each other to never lose sight of the fact that, despite whatever logistical nightmares we encountered, we would be sitting down with every student, in the presence of their parents, adviser, and a peer advocate, to listen as they told us who they were, what they knew, what they wanted to learn, what they felt. That's what motivated us.

Our students were anxious. Similar to our first class of seniors who balked at having to participate in a Senior Project, our sopho-mores threatened not to do the work; they complained about being guinea pigs, about being the subject of an experiment. There were moments of high drama, from kids and from their parents, but in the end, all kids participated. And, of course, by the second year, those pioneers became strong advocates of the Division One Exhibi-tion, meeting with teachers and ninth-graders to introduce the exhibition to them. Kids get hooked on tradition, and now the language of Division One Exhibition is embedded from their first day as ninth-graders.

What We Learn from the Division One Exhibition

The element of student choice in assembling their portfolios provides us with a clear sense of what work matters most to our students; thus teach-ers' work, through the assignments selected by the students for their round-tables, is made public to a larger audience as well. Furthermore, we have designed very specific rubrics for the student presentations. These rubrics clearly describe four possible levels of student achievement. Because the roundtable serves as the culminating exhibition of student work in Divi-sion One, teachers also look at student scores on external assessments, such as the PSATs and the New Hampshire State Assessments, to ensure that teacher assessments of the Division One Exhibition are valid and reliable.

Beyond these objective measures, however, we also learn the value of personalizing learning experiences for our students and their families. All 270 tenth-grade students participate in the Division One Exhibition, and although the elements are the same for all students, their preparation and their experience mirror their individuality.

Student and Family Views. Lyz recognizes that she deliberately sabo-taged all efforts to help her prepare for the Division One Exhibition. Her modus operandi was to slouch, smoke, gossip, cut classes, and fight with every adult in her life. Lyz became annoyed when teachers recognized flashes of brilliance—when she wrote an exquisite line of poetry, or when she became Mayella Ewell in the courtroom scene of *To Kill a Mockingbird*. She was locked in a power struggle with her parents and teachers that prevented her from succeeding in high school. Those of us trying to engage her in her learning were wasting our time; *not* learning was exactly the point. During her first 2 years of high school, her teachers all offered the same comments about Lyz—unlimited potential, but no motivation. Many people tried to encourage Lyz, but they knew that until she worked to resolve her personal conflicts, there was not much they could do. Looking back on her lack of preparation for the Division One Exhibition, Lyz says:

> I didn't want to be in school. It seemed like a waste of my time. I didn't like my adviser, John Dowd. He was just another person trying to help me, an annoyance. I had to deal with him because of the stupid Division One Exhibition, but I wasn't very nice. My boyfriend at the time was a friend of John's, and he kept telling me to be nice to John. Truthfully, no adviser would have made a difference to me, but I focused a lot of anger on John.
>
> The night before my roundtable, I finally saw that I had been a complete jerk. I had the work I needed—it pissed me off when I realized that because I had spent so much time running away from it. The thing that frustrates me most is that I brought most of the bad stuff on myself. Anger almost destroyed me.
>
> I couldn't have done it without my peer advocate. She just kept calming me down. My letter to my roundtable was good because I can write and express myself well, but mostly, I just wanted to get through. And, in the end, I did. I passed.

Lyz's conversation with her panel was difficult; they encouraged her to talk about the poor choices she had made throughout her high school experience. She laughs today as a friend calls her a soap opera, full of high drama and rolling eyes. John Dowd, Lyz's adviser, agrees with Lyz's assessment of her anger:

> Helping Lyz to prepare for her Division One Exhibition was almost impossible. The one saving grace is that we both knew that she would eventually have to sit across a table from me and her parents, and discuss her work. She hated that. I told her that she limited my ability to be her adviser. When questioned about

behavior or missing work, she became very upset and acted badly. It was hard to have a substantive conversation with her because she always walked away, but when I could get her attention, she could acknowledge the truth of what I said. And in all her troubled times, she wasn't driven away from the school. There is good stuff for her here, and at some level, she understands that.

Lyz's mom acknowledges Lyz's growth over the past 2 years. She remembers vividly the days leading up to Lyz's Division One Exhibition.

Lyz was almost paralyzed by nerves as she tried to organize her work. I was struck by the way her friends responded. Her friends were terrific. There was so much activity; the dining room table was covered, the kitchen was filled with Lyz's stuff. Throughout those days, she just kept saying, over and over, that she was not going to make it. But she did.

I remember being blown away by her roundtable. I didn't fully appreciate what it meant to her to have to gather herself like that in front of teachers and parents and her friends. This was so big.

The Division One Exhibition was a high point in a low year for Lyz. She acknowledges that her transcript "looks like crap" and understands that her future is held hostage to the choices she makes. According to her mother, Lyz "has turned the corner and is trying to take charge of herself in a positive way. She knows herself now in a way she never did before."

In contrast to Lyz's experience, Brendan Shea's preparation for the Division One Exhibition was celebratory in nature. An excellent student, Brendan has fully recovered from the childhood leukemia that threatened his life in the seventh and eighth grades. He relishes his close relationships with his family, his teachers, and his friends. When his basketball team traveled north to Hanover, doctors and nurses from Dartmouth's Mary Hitchcock Hospital filled the stands with cheers for their former patient.

Brendan loves to talk about the changes he noticed in his work from his ninth-grade year to his tenth-grade experience. He had always taken a great deal of pride in his work but had often become frustrated when asked to revise his concrete responses to complex topics. He claims that he is "way abstract now." Brendan's wry humor endears him to his classmates and teachers.

Brendan recalls his experience in preparing for the Exhibition.

Until that day, I didn't know how big it would be. We worked hard to assemble the portfolio all year, but until the final presentation, I didn't see how the school really works. You don't usually get a chance to put it all together. Presenting my work and my ideas to Dr. Bob, Kris Gallo, my mom, and a couple of friends was cool. I had planned everything I wanted to say, but as I spoke, I was thinking and questioning myself all the time.

When I first entered high school, I was very black-and-white. I didn't like any gray areas in the ninth grade. My cover letter explained all of that. The only thing I didn't do well on was my level of organization. The conversation with my teachers about how to organize my work made a difference in planning out my Senior Project; I knew I had to listen to people who were trying to help me. I react reluctantly to hearing corrections. Having the chance to review the work I had done over 2 years, however, helped me to reflect on it rather than to react to suggestions to improve it.

Brendan's mom, Katie, agrees with her son's assessment of his work:

Brendan has always been a concrete learner. To him, a horse was a horse was a horse. When he chose to include an abstract drawing instead of a more realistic piece as one of his artifacts in his portfolio, I saw just how far he had come in his thinking. I also was surprised that Brendan was so excited that his principal had been asked to serve on his panel. Instead of being nervous, Brendan knew that Dr. Bob would ask valid questions of Brendan's progress and growth. Brendan had learned to accept other opinions about his work, a necessary step in his growing up. The Division One Exhibition was a very complete event. Brendan used his experiences in preparing this work in his future course selections, in choosing teachers for his junior and senior year, and in planning his Senior Project.

This was my first opportunity to see Brendan present his work, and I was quite surprised. I had seen him rehearse many projects at home, but to see him so articulate, so composed, was very powerful. As a parent, this was my rite of passage as well. Sitting in that room, watching my son speak about the work he has done, what he did not feel good about, what he has learned, how he sees himself as a learner, his goals and objectives, I realized that he was not a child anymore. I saw how he would apply his learning to other experiences. I had to recognize his growth, to acknowledge all that has happened to my son. As I watched Brendan, I realized I was watching a grown-up. I was struck by his honesty as he spoke about what he believed to be just and unjust in his learning experiences. I was not prepared for the power and emotion of this Exhibition.

Unlike Brendan, students such as Jake have a harder path through their high school years. Jake is a very bright young man with a disarming sense of humor and a strong interest in heavy metal music. As the loneliest kid in the ninth grade, Jake knew that his teachers were aware that he had Tourette's syndrome, but Jake would not allow any communication on this topic, and he would not allow any modifications of his assignments. Instead, he worked excruciatingly hard to keep his tics at bay during his schoolday. The price he paid for this diligence was to lose sleep at night, arriving at school each day exhausted and medicated. His mom called his team teachers often when Jake was at his lowest. They met with his psychologist and his medical specialist, extended deadlines, and offered alternative assignments, but Jake would decline all efforts to make his schooldays more manageable. His teachers knew that finding someone to confide in would be a huge step in his acceptance of himself. They were sad to see Jake leave ninth grade in June, knowing that his summer would be a lonely one.

Jake found a friend at the beginning of tenth grade and credited this friendship with helping him develop a strong sense of self-worth. He acquired a girlfriend and, for a while, he completely lost his academic focus, caught up in this powerful new aspect of his life. His teachers were able to connect with Jake, however, and he accepted some modifications of his assignments. In the spring of his sophomore year, Jake presented his research on Tourette's for a final project in biology, acknowledging his personal relationship with this disorder. In speaking about his preparation for the Division One Exhibition, Jake says:

> I got to see the difference it made to let other people help me. I knew that I had to accept help once I left the team structure of Division One. I could see that I had made a lot of changes. I am creative, and I care about my work. In looking at my work, I could see that teachers cared about me.
>
> It hadn't been easy for me to make friends, to let someone know me, but in tenth grade I became friends with someone who helped me to recognize my character traits, things about me that were worthwhile. I found a girlfriend; that was a new experience for me. Both these people helped me a lot. Once I felt that I mattered, I began to be able to know that I was not just my Tourette's, and I knew that I was ready to talk about Tourette's. When I presented my information, nobody teased me or made a big deal about it. I had Tourette's, but I had learned that I was more than a person with a disorder.

Jake's mom worried about his lack of readiness for the roundtable:

Jake was having a difficult time with depression, and his team had extended the due date for his portfolio, but he had been hoping to get out of the roundtable, and they wouldn't let him off the hook for that. His teachers knew that he could talk to his assembled panel about his school experiences, and they held him to that. It was fun to hear Jake's friend describe him as overly social; I laughed at that remark. It was wonderful to have his friend at his roundtable.

My husband's participation in Jake's roundtable was so important. He grew up in a very different educational system and isn't always comfortable in the school. Until that day, I had been the one who maintained contact with the school and managed Jake's education. What was so important about the roundtable was that he sat and listened to Jake and to his responses to the questions his panel asked. A captive audience, he began to understand his son that day. He was very proud of his son, and after that experience, they began to forge a strong connection.

The relationship with his dad was not the only change that affected Jake after his participation in the Division One Exhibition. He began to work with a tutor. His design for the yearbook cover was accepted by his classmates, and he said that he has "learned to appreciate Tourette's because it has forced me to find creative ways to express myself. I am more creative than I would be without the Tourette's. I understand that now."

Faculty Views. For Cathy Fischer-Mueller, the true meaning of the Division One Exhibition is the personalization of the learning process:

Our students sit before us and tell us how they are doing. Imagine that: Adolescents who are often uncomfortable speaking in front of a group, kids who only offer one-syllable answers to adult questions—every single tenth-grade student speaks to an intimate audience and receives personal feedback. Kids step up; they are the only authority in the room because the topic is about self. What an incredible tool we are helping them to develop.

Tenth-grade teachers understand the power of the Division One Exhibition. For math teacher Scott Prescott:

The Division One Exhibition is the best thing we do. The community sees what we value and the kids rise to the occasion. I want us to use the Exhibition as a way to strengthen the Division One experience for students, to question what we are teaching and what is important for us.

For Scott, the "aha" moment comes most frequently for the quiet students who don't speak up in class. "To be a part of that conversation, to listen to them describe themselves, that is the power of the moment." Scott wishes he could harness the energy of these presentations. He regrets that the presentations signal the end of the year.

Chris Balch, science teacher and wilderness leader, knows that for one of his students, the end of the schoolyear is his only good news:

On an adventure to the Rockies, this boy was a star; he smiled constantly, and his body language conveyed authority and fulfillment, but he was sad when he talked about himself as a student. He acknowledged that sadness during his Division One Exhibition. Unfortunately, his realization that he did not perform well as a ninth- or tenth-grader did not empower him to improve. He recognized that, however. He understands his responsibility for his lack of success, and he doesn't deny his actions. He doesn't blame his problems on anyone else. He isn't very good at school, but in the mountains, this kid shines.

Chris believes that helping his students prepare their portfolios teaches him about what matters most to his students. "I realized that one of my advisees spent a lot of her life on the ballet stage. She had experienced success as a dancer. I was able to build on that knowledge of her in my class."

Anne Clifton-Waite became a convert to the Division One Exhibition after a rough first year with the process:

Tom and Cathy had seen roundtables in action during their trip to New York, but I could not imagine what they would be like. I felt that it was a lot to ask of teachers. I also had questions about the assessment piece. Logistically, it was tough, and I am not very process-oriented. But the truth is that the logistics get easier, and, fortunately, someone always steps up to organize the rest of us. For me, the moment of truth came when I participated in the roundtables. Oh, there are a few we worry about—an occasional parent who balks at the concept, or a few kids who drag their feet, but there is always that moment of self-awareness that leads to new understanding.

I have participated in a wide range of student engagement. Perhaps the student who has stayed in my mind the most is a boy who was not going to pass his courses for the year. Melissa Chapman attended this particular roundtable, and she really pushed the boy with her questions. He mentioned that he planned to take her course in conservation biology, and after the roundtable, she brought him to her classroom and showed him the work he would be doing. She extended herself to demonstrate that she would be willing to help him but that she would also demand much from him. That was a special moment.

Students Who Do Not Succeed

For students who have not completed the criteria for the Division One Exhibition, the roundtable takes on a particular sense of urgency. The roundtable serves as a genuine wake-up call because it is taking place at the same moment that his or her peers are celebrating their successful passage. Students who do not pass their Division One Exhibition attend summer school to complete the work. When they have completed the requirements, they repeat their roundtable and present their portfolio. We have scheduled roundtables for students as late as the fall or winter of their junior year. This is high-stakes testing in its most authentic form. The student who re-presents has not crammed for a test; teachers have not supplied last year's multiple-choice questions. Instead, the student has worked to document his progress in meeting our learner expectations, and his teachers, parents, and peers are there to witness his achievement.

It is evident that tenth-grade teachers have begun to build upon the initial work of the Division One Exhibition and to explore its value as a teaching and learning tool. In discussing the Exhibition's possible use as a gateway for students, Scott Prescott says, "We have been successful at using the preparation for the Division One Exhibition as a way to identify and catch kids who are slipping, but we should resist the notion of having one mechanism stop kids from moving forward."

The Implications of the Exhibition

There are many layers of learning embedded in this process. First, the Division One Exhibition succeeds because we make a considerable investment in knowing our students well. Teachers have provided significant academic challenges and expectations to ensure that all of their students, in a heterogeneous context, meet high standards. Throughout the process, students receive regular academic support from teachers who routinely discuss students' needs during the team's common planning time. Advisers, in turn, have nurtured and nudged their students to reflect on their learning and on their academic futures. Along the way, advisers discover the many dimensions of these individuals and are able to discuss the tricky balancing act of adolescence. The presence of powerful grown-ups in their school lives offers students positive models to help them navigate through the maze from childhood to that of independent self.

As a "ritual [that] translates[s] the invisible movement going on inside an adolescent into an external event so all can share in it" (Oldfield, p. xiv), the Division One Exhibition meets the accepted criteria of a societal rite of passage—a time to reflect, a difficult challenge, caring mentors, a witnessing and acknowledgment of accomplishment, and a moving on.

As Brendan Shea's mom points out, the Division One Exhibition also serves to make explicit the parents' work in helping their child reach this moment and to highlight the coming change in the nature of the parent–child relationship.

Beyond the import of the occasion, the roundtable also serves as a transition from the structured team environment of the ninth and tenth grades to a more individualized Division Two experience. The presence of Division Two teachers at the roundtable underscores this transition.

Ninth-grade teachers play a similar role to those of the parents at the roundtable. They have been responsible for introducing students to Souhegan's Mission Statement and to all the programs and policies of the high school. These teachers served as a guide during their initial struggles. Attending the roundtables allows ninth-grade teachers to recognize the significant academic and emotional growth of their former students and to provide a show of personal support one more time.

Cathy Fischer-Mueller represents the thoughts of many colleagues when she stresses the importance of sitting and listening to students reflect on their learning halfway through their high school careers. However, as important as the roundtable has become as a culmination of the Division One Exhibition, the student portfolios themselves have come to represent Souhegan's real Rosetta Stone. For students, portfolios serve as the collective body of academic successes and failures over 2 years of their lives. For the school, however, they are much more than that. Sophomore portfolios have become a collective representation of Souhegan's own successes and failures, providing a wealth of data to the academic community. The portfolios do the following:

- Provide strong evidence of what students value because they have sifted through 2 years of work in every discipline to identify that work which best demonstrates their acquisition of skills and knowledge.

- Help us discern whether our assessments have really worked—and whether they are sophisticated enough to show us that students have achieved proficiency in our learner expectations.
- Provide a mechanism to explore the relationship between our schoolwide Learner Expectations and student achievement on the New Hampshire State Assessment.
- Help to refine the alignment of curriculum scope and sequence in grades 7–10, the grades tested by the New Hampshire State Assessment.
- Help to establish clearer benchmarks for knowledge, skills, and habits that students demonstrate in performance tasks that they choose to include.
- Assist us in developing rigorous standards in our curriculum and assessment.
- Provide a key communication link between ninth- and tenth-grade teachers.
- Provide a way to document both our beliefs and our practices with respect to teaching and learning at Souhegan High School.

Cathy Fischer-Mueller says,

In the past, my work and my comments about my students' work was strictly between the two of us. Now, my work and my assessment of student performance is opened to all who read my students' portfolios. This makes me more aware, more thoughtful on a daily basis, and more accountable to my colleagues, my students, and their parents.

Cathy's thoughts reveal an essential aspect of this initiative, the foundation of a strong professional community. In preparing students for this work, her colleagues demonstrate collegiality, innovation, adult learning, commitment to success for all students, and high standards.

Souhegan High School has almost doubled its size since its opening in September of 1992, and we all point to our rapid growth as being the enemy of sustained conversation about essential elements of reform. In an ever-changing environment, it is increasingly hard to cut through the clutter of concerns competing for time. However, Lyz's father offers a reminder as to why we do this work.

In the Division One Exhibition, I found that the school managed to make itself small on this occasion. Here was a large institution that had become quite intimate, devoting the time and energy to listen to students, to critique their work, and to evaluate the entire process. Despite its size, the school delivered important individual attention to each of its tenth-grade students. I was impressed by that.

The Division One Exhibition does not serve as the sole marker of student achievement. As coordinator Melanie Gallo discusses in the next section, the Senior Project offers students another opportunity to demonstrate a high standard of performance in this culminating assessment of their high school experience.

SENIOR PROJECT,
BY MELANIE GALLO

I am sitting in the theater watching Meghan Kirkwood present her Senior Project. I am late and as a result I am in the last row in the balcony—I have the entire audience beneath me, quietly concentrating on Meghan's calm, competent delivery of her expertise as she grapples with the questions "How Is Photography Art?" and "Am I an Artist?"

Perhaps it's the darkness in the theater. Perhaps it's the rapt attention of the audience. Perhaps it is Meghan softly telling us what she has yet to learn. But I am warmed by the love and caring present in the moment, in this space, for this rite of passage.

In the beginning was the word and the word was that we didn't know what we were doing. And the word was the truth. The senior seminar team had been charged with creating an exhibition that would serve as a graduation requirement and that would demonstrate skills implicit in the meaning of Souhegan High School's diploma. The task was daunting. Our senior class had transferred from the neighboring town when Souhegan opened, and they were reluctant—actually, they were downright resistant—to the concept of Senior Project. When I look back at the original packet that we created, literally one page ahead of when it would be needed, I can't believe how far we've come.

In 1992, when Souhegan High School was about to open its doors, the staff came together for a brief 3-week period in late August. I met for the first time the three men who would serve with me as senior seminar teachers. Senior seminar was to be an interdisciplinary experience for all seniors, co-taught by two teachers. We would use as our focus questions: Who am I? What do I believe? And How can I make a difference in the world? English was to be the subject paired with social studies or science. This seminar would also orchestrate a unique, independent learning experience to be called Senior Project. This project was to be designed and implemented primarily by the four of us, although we quickly discovered that lots of the staff wanted to be involved in the planning. Twenty or 30 individuals, each with a multitude of interesting and exciting thoughts, attended our initial meetings. Membership in a new initiative is crucial, but in order to move from concept to product, we had to limit the decision makers. Since ultimately the seminar would oversee the project, the four of us (seminar teachers) took charge. We piloted this project with 118 students, but on that maiden voyage were also another 100 adults who served as mentors.

As we prepared our own unique design, we investigated other culminating projects at other high schools as well. Most were "owned" by the English departments, and we wanted a broader scope. We also recognized that the parameters of such an exhibition needed to fit our student population and our community. We constantly asked ourselves what we wanted for *our* students and how such an exhibition could support *their* learning needs.

We wanted them engaged in learning, we wanted them to develop skills that connected them to the world outside school, we wanted them to become active members of their community, and we wanted them to take ownership for their personal growth. How could one project fit so many requirements and still retain its creative core? How could we make this manageable, hold students accountable, and still not become overly prescriptive? From the beginning, we wanted to control quality, not passion. And so began our birthing process.

The first place we looked for inspiration was to our school's Mission Statement. It had to be the heart of whatever we created. We wanted to make education meaningful in a personalized way. To engage hearts, minds, and passions was critical.

What Is Senior Project?

Senior Project is an active research project in which students choose a topic of interest, something that they really want to learn more about. They read about it, they research it, they interview people, and they choose an expert in the area and have conversations. Students choose an essential question, or an inquiry topic, and engage in a process in which all learners work to become an expert. Students have to demonstrate application, to show that they can use this knowledge in a new context. For example, shortly after the bombing of the Federal Building in Oklahoma City, one senior told her mentor that the bombing could not have been the work of foreign terrorists because of the chemicals involved. This senior had become an expert in the field of forensic science.

We give the Senior Project packets out in October. The packet establishes the minimum expectations:

- There will be at least 60 hours of active documented research time.
- Active research will include written notes resulting from personal interaction with human resources, such as a formal interview, internship, apprenticeship, and shadowing of or with an expert on the topic of the project.
- Active research will include the use of printed resources, including books, technical literature, and appropriate articles from reputable sources.
- All deadlines and appointments with mentors, advisers, or others associated with the project will be met.
- Notes from printed resources will include more than just highlighted or underlined passages and must contain a personal synthesis of relevant information.
- An annotated bibliography must include a minimum of 10 citations from a variety of sources.
- There will be at least two thoughtful and dated entries in the learning narrative each week from the beginning of the project to the end.
- All narrative entries documenting the learning process will be word-processed.
- The project binder will be organized according to guidelines and will properly reflect active research.

All students must seek the assistance of an outside expert—a professional in the specified area of research, not a parent, guardian, or faculty member. Students must document frequent contact with this expert, either in person, over the telephone, or through e-mail and/or the Internet.

Students seeking Honors recognition for their work must declare their intentions in their proposal. The guidelines for Honors are the following:

- All deadlines and obligations for project are met.
- All binder checks exceed expectations.
- Presentation is superior, based on a particular set of rubrics provided to the students in their packets.
- Reflection paper is superior.
- The project clearly exhibits that the student has pushed "beyond comfortable limits," as stated in Souhegan's Mission Statement.

The packet also contains assessment criteria for each stage of the project and samples of each required segment. Every student keeps a binder with sections for notes, articles, interviews, and narratives. The narratives track the progress of student thinking, the shifting questions, the frustrations, the threads of new knowledge. This is the section of active learning, of the growth and development of expertise.

During the first stage of the project, students formulate a proposal to present to the Senior Project team. This team works with each student to make sure that the work fits the framework of the project. Often, students will propose a topic for which there is very little research available or propose a very big idea that has no specific details attached. In 8 years, however, we have turned down only one project topic—beer-making (not because it lacked research merit, but because it was inconsistent with our drug and alcohol policies).

This stage of the work is crucial to the project's success. First, students write a letter of intent to a potential mentor detailing the topic they plan to explore. Their mentors are members of the teaching, administrative, custodial, secretarial, or support staff who commit to spending at least half an hour each week with their senior from November through April. Mentors may choose to work with as many as three seniors. Students also contact an outside expert who volunteers to provide guidance for the work. We provide assistance for those seniors who have difficulty finding a mentor or an outside expert. We experimented with having a mentor as an option for students but learned that the student–mentor relationship is an essential component for this work.

Next, the proposal itself is presented to the Senior Project team. Once they have approved the project, senior advisers monitor the progress of their advisees' projects. They check their advisees' binder every 2 weeks through April and maintain contact with their advisee's mentor when necessary. To ensure quality control, the advisers participate in some collective binder checks to calibrate this experience, similar to holistic scoring approaches used by testing organizations. There are periodic "flag days," alerting parents that students are not keeping up with the necessary research or mentor meetings. Once the criteria for having assembled a successful binder have been met, the student receives a date for the public presentation.

Every student must do a 20-minute presentation of his or her topic, with an emphasis on research. Students present their work to a panel comprised of their mentor, their adviser, and their senior seminar teachers. Occasionally, their outside expert sits on the panel as well. The audience usually consists of their fellow Advisory members, parents, friends, other students and teachers, siblings, and community members. The panel uses a rubric to assess the student's presentation skills. Students are asked to compress 60 hours of research and analysis into 20 minutes. We impress on them their responsibility to help their audience understand the topic. It is a critical skill to help someone understand a new idea. We ask them to use presentation media that will enhance their work, and so students frequently use video, PowerPoint, music, slides, and so forth.

Following the presentation, students engage in 10 minutes of questions from the panel and the audience. This is a very powerful experience for students in the audience, as well as for the presenter and the audience. The presenter must be prepared for a wide range of questions, often questions that allow him to demonstrate a broader knowledge of the topic. The audience will frequently ask the presenter to summarize his essential questions or review the application of research, all to help the presenter strengthen his work. The heart of our Mission Statement proclaims that we are a community of learners, and nothing demonstrates that as much as the collegiality that emerges during a presentation.

After the presentation, the panel convenes immediately, reviews the rubric, and assembles detailed feedback for the presenter. The panel then calls the student to sit with them and review the feedback. Students know immediately whether they have passed this part of their project. They do not pass if they have not rehearsed their presentation or demonstrated organized thought during their presentation. They do not pass if their research is incomplete.

The final stage of the project is the completion of a six- to eight-page reflection paper. We ask students to reflect on the "habits of mind" that they used during the course of their research and on what they now know about themselves as learners. Our students have practiced reflective learning for their 4 years with us; this is their final opportunity to synthesize that learning at Souhegan. This is the place where academic rigor and the affective domain converge. That is where learning hopefully becomes integral to the student's being as a "lifelong learner."

We ask them to weave the Mission Statement into their reflections, an important connection both for them and for the school. How have they developed their "unique gifts, passions, and intentions"? How have they expanded their "comfortable limits of thought, tolerance, and performance"? How have they honored the "active stewardship of family, nation, and globe"? How have they exhibited "courage" in their learning? We know the power of the Mission Statement in students' lives; this final reflection provides an "aha" moment. Students discover that they have become the embodiment of this document. The reflection papers speak to the heart of who we are as a school and what we have passed on to our students.

During the week following completion of Senior Project, we ask the community to attend an evening of Senior Project presentations, culminating with an awards ceremony. We call attention to those students who have demonstrated significant personal growth, students whose research has been exemplary, students whose presentations have wowed their audience, students who have reflected most thoughtfully on their work. One highlight of this evening is a presentation by Amherst resident Ann Bergin of cash awards to three students whose work was exemplary. As a lasting honor to an aunt who valued education, Ann has also presented a plaque that lists the award winners each year.

The Rest of the Story

The Senior Project is an opportunity given to kids to discover the pure joy of learning for its own sake. That joy is always colored by the organizational piece, but students are most successful when they get lost in the work, when the work soars past any required documentation.

During our first year, we were only one page ahead of the kids, every single step of the project. We were making it up as we went along—and it showed. We knew that we would be an exhibition-based school and that the Senior Project would be the culminating exhibition. That first class challenged us regarding their participation. They asked Dr. Bob what would happen if they simply did not complete the work. His response, delivered in all good humor, was how lonely it would be at graduation without them. That turned the tide, and the kids buckled down.

During the second year, we developed our rationale for the work, and the students understood the rationale, and their work demonstrated their commitment. To connect with kids' passions is the heart of Senior Project, and so we have traveled to backyards to see a hand-built forge; we have swatted mosquitoes as we have observed equestrian demonstrations; we have watched students learn to fly-fish, to build a geodesic dome, to write stories, to compose music, to build kayaks, to direct plays, to climb mountains, to seek solitude. We see the pride and the joy of a student becoming an expert.

We want students to reach out to others, to learn from others. We encourage them to use the phone, to contact college professors via e-mail, to track down sources, to call back, to manage time, to reschedule, to write letters, to network. These are life skills that extend far beyond the scope of school. This is active research and applied learning at its best.

The most successful projects explore students' interests. Each year, some parents will try to push their child to study a particular topic, but we tell the kids that if the parents want to do a Senior Project, we will issue them a binder. The work is too hard not to be born of natural curiosity.

Kara Laing's ('98) curiosity led her to explore Gypsy culture. A dancer, she studied the flamenco as an artistic form of expression for that culture.

She learned the dance, made her costume, and gave a flamenco performance. She developed her passion; it left the project and went off on its own to the highest level of exploration.

The need to complete his Senior Project provided Kevin Donovan ('00) with the catalyst to develop his passion for writing and art. He wrote a mystery novel set in a museum in Manchester and is now pursuing publication of his work.

Dan Ward ('00) presented a landscaping plan that includes stone walls. When describing his work as a stone mason, Dan talks about the "flow" of the work. He says, sounding much like Robert Frost, "There is something about a wall . . ."

Senior Project gives all kinds of kids a chance to be acknowledged as an expert among their peers. One student musician created such a buzz with his junk band that everybody talked about it for days. He had made a drum set out of found objects. One student convinced us of her future as a business magnate with her business plan for a water theme park; when she seeks investors, she will find them in her former high school teachers. One student asked the question of whether God truly exists and sought to answer the question through the work of two philosophers. Her narratives as she explored the question showed intense learning. One young woman studied the oppression of Middle Eastern women and wrote poetry filled with rage and tears on this topic.

Adults have offered amazing expertise to our students. A New York DJ worked with Gayle Willis via e-mail, then traveled to New Hampshire to attend her presentation. Author Ray Bradbury wrote a graceful letter to Kerry Silva, who had requested his assistance during her project, and sent her autographed copies of his own work. An animator with Disney helped one of our student animators create a series of sophisticated computer animations through almost-daily e-mail advice.

We have many quiet triumphs. Learning specialist Amanda Wood discusses the work of one of her seniors:

> Matt is a student with Down syndrome who has highly developed social skills. He relates well to other kids, and they enjoy him. Last year he led a cheer during a schoolwide pep rally, and everybody responded to Matt.
>
> For his Senior Project, Matt studied what it takes to be a coach; he did a phenomenal job. We broke the work into manageable chunks for him. Practicing his cursive writing, he sent 10 letters to coaches, asking to interview them for his project. He developed interview questions and practiced his interview skills with several teachers. He also wrote to the Mighty Ducks hockey team and was

overwhelmed when he received a reply—eight Mighty Ducks T-shirts and a book. A local hockey rink donated ice time so that Matt could coach a game between Souhegan High School and Trinity High School in Manchester. Matt met every checkpoint, and his work was exemplary. Matt was proud because the work asked of him was the same work that was asked of every senior. He organized his work, conducted authentic research, worked with an outside expert, applied his research, and reflected on the meaning of his work. I was very proud of his success. As someone who has dealt with the effects of my own dyslexia, I truly understand what it means to meet a challenge and surpass expectations.

We cry, often, when we watch our students step up to their work. One young woman was an in-your-face kind of kid, very willing to tell teachers what was wrong in their classrooms, but when it was time for her project, she rehearsed 30 or 40 times in front of anyone she could convince to watch her. She had taken a course through a social service agency and had become certified as a court advocate for victims of abuse. Her project was flawless, and at the end, she burst into tears. Her work stays in my mind.

One student studied teen pregnancy and was invited to meet the governor. One nonverbal student presented his work on a computer. One young man shouted angrily that we had not accepted his presentation because of his learning disabilities. We told him that he had not passed because he had not met our expectations of him. He began to work again and visited the Big Dig construction site in Boston to learn more about bridge building, and when he re-presented his work, he almost could not contain his excitement about his learning.

Occasionally, a student travels to explore a topic. Students can apply for Senior Project research days, similar to professional development days for teachers. This year, Senior Project came full circle when a student traveled to Florida to do some dolphin research and met a researcher who was a former Souhegan graduate who had traveled to Hawaii to study dolphins for her Senior Project.

In their work, students often explore important young adult themes. They have studied their families' stories and have discovered themselves. One student began with a very vague idea of doing something on twins, and as time went by, he narrowed his focus to his own relationship as a twin and finally to question whether he, indeed, really was an identical twin. His final question asked what it would mean for his own identity at 18 if he discovered that he was a fraternal, not an identical, twin. A young woman wrote a book, *65 Roses*, about her sister's death from cystic fibrosis; another searched her family history to learn more about her Vietnamese mother and American father. Over the years, we forget some students' names, but we remember all of them by their Senior Project.

Sometimes it is in struggle and in adversity that we meet our true selves. Nowhere is this more evident than in the students who struggle with their Senior Project. They are an interesting palette of personalities. They are not a group easily categorized. When I sit down to review their project binders, there is a unique story behind each. One student has fallen victim to a difficult divorce, another to dependency on alcohol, and yet another is immobilized by the fear of graduating and leaving high school for the unknown. Drugs, homelessness, procrastination, and simple or not-so-simple lack of motivation all play a part. The pain and pleasure of this project is that it asks students to challenge themselves in ways that they have never done. Every student can choose to succeed, but the choice is not always an easy one.

Behind every example of students who struggle is a cadre of adults whose work surrounds this effort. One senior boy who planned to study avalanches was buried by his own avalanche of neglect for his coursework and his Senior Project. His teachers alerted his adviser; his adviser alerted members of his panel and his mentor; his mentor, his adviser, and his teachers spoke to his parents; the principal met with him to establish a game plan; his mentor met with another colleague to polish an essential question. His basketball coach monitored the conversations. Every adult communicated their strategies to the student and to each other; their efforts eventually succeeded in getting this young man unstuck. Senior Project requires the collaboration of many individuals.

Senior Project is a life lesson. For us the stakes are tremendously high, and so we work very carefully with each troubled case. We continue to let the students know that we are champions for their success but that we will hold them to the standards of the project. Sometimes, students struggling through their coursework make choices as to whether to complete Senior Project or to give their energies to their academic subjects. They accept that they must do both before they can graduate. As the day nears for students to have a presentation date assigned, binders are checked and research is approved.

Some students' work is judged not ready for presentation. If we believe that this work is about process, we cannot support a learning log that has been created in the last 2 weeks of the project. If it were possible to become an expert in 2 weeks, that would be the length of the entire project. We (the principal, mentor, and myself) begin a series of meetings with each student. Each student's parent receives a letter informing him or her that their son or daughter is in danger of not graduating. A new date for the presentation is assigned. The student is then expected to create a plan that sets goals and deadlines in order to meet the new date. On the assigned date, the student comes with the research binder and explains how the goals have been met.

Some students meet their goals, successfully present, and carefully reflect on what caused the problems in the first place. Others still can't get the work done. For these students, conversations often involve tears and the sad realization that graduation will be delayed. Interestingly enough, there isn't a lot of anger. More often than not there is honesty about what hasn't happened. It is important to note that even at this point, for these students, we are not finished. Support remains and students come back in June, July, and August to present and finally earn a diploma. Some of our greatest successes have occurred the following January. In the end, their diploma from Souhegan High School matters a great deal, and we know that the students not ready to leave us in June will continue to be surrounded by caring adults until they have demonstrated this culminating exhibition of knowledge and skills. It is our firm resolve to hold students accountable and to show them that often in failure we discover the depth of our possibility.

The Challenges We Face

The tension now is that we are trying to do with 220 students the same work that we did with an original 118. We no longer have 4 seminar teachers serving as proctors; there are now 21 advisers overseeing the work. Several senior advisers are new to Souhegan and have never observed a Senior Project or mentored a student. Consequently, people want more safety nets, more paperwork to track the process. The larger we get, the more complicated it becomes to administer the project. In our stress of space, time, and numbers, we must avoid missing the point that Senior Project has to be a rich conversation with adults about learning and about ideas.

We need to help adults become more confident. We have learned over and over and over that when there is personalization, when there is authenticity, there is a connection. We know that the best start to a Senior Project is to have the student, mentor, and Senior Project team meet to fine-tune the proposal, make suggestions, and tighten the idea. We do not shuffle paper; we meet with kids. It is labor-intensive and exhausting work, but ultimately rewarding. The students have a heightened sense of creative tension as they present their ideas to the adults who must help them succeed. They see, hear, and feel the intensity of the work they are about to begin, and it elevates the work.

This year the adults balked at the number of hours this process consumes, and so we collected student proposals and passed them back and forth to each other and to and from the student. The result was that we all noticed less seriousness of intent from many of our students this year; they are missing the creative tension that is essential to begin the work and treat it with respect. We may be making choices that don't support the work. Perhaps they are necessary choices, given the constraints of our environment, but they are choices that are troubling to all of us.

Stress levels are high for our students and for the teachers most involved with Senior Project, and we need to address this. If we restructured the schoolday, we could offer a mandatory elective on the Senior Project that would give students time each day to work on their project and time for the adults to monitor their progress. We are facing an ultimate test of our beliefs. If the Senior Project is critical, if it is the culmination of a process that results in a Souhegan diploma, then we need to honor the time required to do the work.

The Value of the Work

In the end, we know that when we honor student expertise and work on such a scale, in such a public way, it is worth all our effort. Senior Project is about more than requirements and deadlines. It is about more than finding a mentor and choosing a topic. It is about more than applied research and public performance. It is at its very soul about passion, the passion that comes from deep connection and personal struggle, from introspection and growth. It is, as most education is, about story. The stories are as unique as each student, and after 8 years, they number nearly 1,000. These stories include the following.

To find an answer as to why his eye surgery limited his skills at baseball, a game he loved, one student worked with one of the pioneer physicians in sports vision therapy.

One student focused her research on her own atrial septal defect condition, a condition that required her to have surgery at the beginning of her senior year. She videotaped her operation as a start to her research, definitely pushing my comfortable limits, and worked with the doctors who helped her. I can still see her standing with her pointer during her presentation saying, "This is when they stopped my heart." At that moment, mine did also.

One young woman started out asking why a specific gene mutated and caused her particular condition, eventually discovering that what she really wanted to know was how to help people cope with this condition. She set up a national network for patients and presented her findings to doctors at Boston Children's Hospital.

One student's research and paper on the behavioral characteristics of monkeys was accepted for presentation at a national science forum.

One senior trained for and ran the Boston Marathon.

One senior worked to find a way to improve conditions for the women of Afghanistan.

A year after presenting a film in the comedic style of Buster Keaton that he had written, directed, and produced, one graduate was awarded highest honors in a New Hampshire film contest.

To overcome her fear of spiders, one senior studied phobias and hypnosis.

Much to the delight of his audience, one young man turned himself into a one-man band to demonstrate his knowledge of percussion.

One senior demonstrated his knowledge of pyrotechnics by producing an amazing fireworks display at graduation.

Senior Project Reflections

After the research, the meetings, the binder checks, and the presentation, after the procrastination, the angst, and final fruition, there is reflection. Of course, students have reflected throughout the experience, but now we ask them to assess the integrity of their process and to connect their growth to the Souhegan Mission Statement. Our students have used the Mission Statement to assess their learning each year, but this last reflection is the culmination of 4 years of hard work. To guide their final Senior Project assignment, due 5 days after the successful completion of their presentation, we ask them to consider the following questions:

- What have you discovered about your ability to plan and to solve problems?
- How do you intend to use the knowledge and skills that you have gained?
- What have you discovered about your own thinking?
- What have you learned to value about yourself in this process?
- What aspects of the Mission Statement does your project reflect?

The rigor of Senior Project has become evident. The reflections offer us a window into some of the intangibles of the work. Seniors experience this work together, and they bond together as a class in ways that they would in few other schools. They rehearse with their Advisory and incorporate their friends' feedback into their presentation. They teach each other how to use technology to improve their presentation and how to speak to an audience. They support each other's work—they help set up the room beforehand; they calm each other down and pump each other up. They ask thoughtful questions, and they enthusiastically applaud. They wait anxiously until the panel announces that the student has passed the presentation phase of the Senior Project, and they celebrate with hugs and shouts. They recognize the importance of the work.

Many presentations leave us in awe of the personal growth of the presenter. We have selected three reflection papers from the class of 2000 to demonstrate individual journeys. Meghan Kirkwood articulates her pride in watching her friends' projects and gives us a clear sense of the depth of her questions as she attempted to respond to her essential question involving photography and the creative process.

Kenneth Bailey was fascinated with his learning during his Senior Project. He chose to research childhood leukemia, a disease he had survived at the age of 3.

Lyz Trainor offers a different perspective of the work. Everybody in the building was aware of Lyz's stress as she battled herself to succeed. Her presentation wowed her audience, but her reflection reveals her growing knowledge of herself.

The Senior Project, in its entirety, is much more than the students' culminating performance. It provides the opportunity for all who have worked with our students to see, hear, and feel their arrival at the end of their adolescence and the beginning of their adult lives. To read their reflections is to know they are ready to leave us.

Meghan Kirkwood. I began this project with the expectation that it would cause me to grow; I knew it was going to be difficult, beautiful and emotional. I was sure that these feelings would be the result of my own process, and they were. However, I did not expect that emotional demands would come from other projects and experiences, and challenge me as much as the ones from my own did. Before I address the change and growth that I have undergone as a result of my project, I would like to talk about the unexpected effects that this project, holistically, has had on me as a learner and human being.

I did not realize that I had been affected until this afternoon. I watched Hillary present and I started to cry in the last five minutes of her presentation, and she was only explaining how she bound her book. I thought I was crying because she went into her presentation so nervous, she closed off her presentation to only five friends and a few adults, and she presented so beautifully. She was so nervous, but as soon as she began it was everything I love about Hillary up in front of the room, telling us about her book of her journey, her passion and life. I thought that I was crying because she overcame her fear of failure, a true stretch of her comfortable limits, but this was not why I was crying. Hillary exemplified the most incredible aspect of this project for me, the exhibition of self. I feel my own project and presentation definitely exhibited myself as much as my work, but it was my reflection on the work of my friends and their presentations that instigated this realization.

This was apparent to me as we discussed the Senior Project in her car afterwards. I remember commenting to Hillary that the presentations of our friends almost mirrored perfectly who they are. Lindsay's showed her organization and her perfectionism, Matt's showed his focus, diligence and over-rehearsal, and Kevin's showed his intelligence and complexity. We noted that during each presentation that we saw, we could envision the speaker working on that thing or subject that they love, with a different kind of energy that came naturally to them in the absence of restrictive purpose. As though having invested so much time in something that they were so passionate about had caused us to associate that one thing to be synonymous with them. Each, by presenting their project and this one thing, were indirectly presenting themselves, and for that one span of time, I saw what beautiful, passionate people my friends are. That is why I was crying.

As I consider this and read over the comments that my audience gave to me, I am more flattered and speechless than ever before. If this project is a reflection of myself, can I be described as passionate and reflective? If I can be described this way, was it not exemplified by my exhibition and was it not this project that brought it out in me? I believe that my project on photography as art is synonymous with myself; the time that I invested into a topic so dear to my person and its success speak to the validity of photography written on the space next to my name. Clearly, my audience viewed my project as the concrete connection and instigator between me and honest motivation, passion and experience; as though they saw me kaleidoscope through my project, and attributed this portrayal to my effort towards and love for photography. Was it for this reason that my good friend wrote 'good luck with photography in the future, I think it's given you a lot.' My best friend wrote only one word, 'passion.' Is this why when I saw her presentation all I could do was cry?

It seems to me that this project was ideal; it allowed my friends and myself to present ourselves through a safe, yet revealing process. It differed from our Division One Exhibitions because students who could not invest themselves in their progress could invest in their interest, and subconsciously challenge themselves. I think that this project is Souhegan's great victory, for students, who began their career dismissing the Mission Statement as a bunch of bologna, myself included, to be led almost blindly down a course of their choice and come out thinking of the statement differently. Please do not mistake my imagery to be a lack of sincerity, I honestly believe that this project was an excellent way to challenge both the unmotivated and motivated students. The motivated took on harder projects and surprised themselves that they did it, and the unmotivated can marvel at what they did in the course of meeting minimum expectations. I have never respected my classmates more than I did going to their presentations.

I think that this project is the most intense piece of work that I have ever done at Souhegan. I remember thinking at one point that if I disciplined myself to work for one hour each day on my Senior Project, then I would remain much more on track. I also remember wondering why coming up with my presentation was so tiring; why was I mentally exhausted from talking about art with my father? The answer is that I put everything I had into my project, and as I grew into it, I put in even more of myself to meet my own expectations. I couldn't have spent an equal amount of time on my project each day, it required my full attention and I discovered that that could not be regulated. I spent as much as four hours of continuous time in the darkroom some days and others I spent perplexed at the purpose of surrealism. I am reminded of a quote about an idea "robust enough" to keep you restless.

Photography and art drove me in a similar way; for the first time in my life I was faced with something that I couldn't answer or define, but I knew them so intimately. I felt young, inarticulate, and helpless, but strangely serene, guided by the affirmation that somehow I understood. I have never thought so hard in my life; I was forced by my requirements, driven by my passion and inquiry, and perplexed by my futile attempts to combine and apply what I already knew. This project required more than I already knew, and had it not been my physical and mental self combined, I would have completed this project, but it would not have been a reflection of myself.

The presentation component was one of the most difficult parts of the project, or rather the preparation for my presentation. I rewrote my presentation four times. I practiced about six times and three of those times I went over thirty-five minutes, twice on the twenty-five mark. I could not decide what I wanted to say. Part of the problem with my project was that I had gone through such a transformation and revelation that I wanted to take my audience through my thought process. I wanted them to relive this discovery with me, so they could understand how photography is art without having to go through the extra fifteen typed pages of reflection I did. I was so proud of what I'd done that I wanted everyone to see what had captured my life and my eye. I reminded myself of a small child, fascinated by her sand castle, out of breath as she tells of the dragon that hides under the bridge. On a greater level, I thought that my project proved my intelligence, passion and heart, qualities I always felt I had to defend because I am often in the company of incredible people. Completing a project on something that I love, and presenting with every bit of passion and dedication I had, appropriately solidified my place as neither super-smart nor super-artistic, but rather intelligent and artistic in a different, distinctive way that I can only identify as myself. This is how I would like my peers to remember me.

When I think of the completion of this project, I am left feeling oddly indecisive. I feel that having undergone as many changes as I have, both slight and significant, I should be left with a larger sense of epiphany, but I am not. Yet, I feel fulfilled. This project has been a beginning, not a revelation. I have new ideas of my capabilities, thought, and performance. I do have a new view of myself, one that I see through the sunglasses of my project. Although it provides the strength of example to me as I leave for a place where I am unknown, yet, I know that I am young, and development of self is continuous, in much the same way as the artist. For one moment it is all clear, like the good exhibit, the next it is part of the larger picture of my journey becoming a passionate life-long learner.

Kenneth Bailey. When I first started this paper, I didn't know what topic I should choose. I made a list of topics that would pique my interest, and chose the best one. I came up with childhood leukemia because I owed it to myself to study my own dreaded disease that I once had when I was three. I knew it was going to be a difficult subject to study, mentally and physically, but my interest overcame all that, and brought me through it. I began looking into childhood leukemia in books and web sites, just getting the little descriptions of what leukemia really is. I learned most of my whole project within the first 2–3 weeks of research. I went from library to library reading all the information I could on childhood leukemia. I stayed up till 3 o'clock in the morning researching on my project. And now when I look at how hard I have worked on this project, I realized I did the one thing I never thought I could do, work my hardest! I was shocked and my parents were speechless with the work I had done. As my work went on, I tried harder and harder to teach myself my missing life that was erased from my memory at such a young age. Some of the information I discovered, scared me, and made me nervous. What scared me was all the pain I remembered when I went through the treatments. When I read it out of another person's words and what they went through, I got visions in my mind and it actually helped me remember how it was in the hospital bed and what my family went through while I was suffering from this cancer.

I have discovered that I can do something if I really work hard at it. I proved to myself that I can stand up in front of 30 people, and give a great presentation without passing out, or becoming nauseous. All my life, I was always helped out on doing these projects, and I thought I would never make it alone. Mary Young, my case manager, was my mentor for this project, and about two weeks before presentation, she told me that she never helped me out that much, I basically did this all on my own, and I didn't believe it, until I sat down and thought about it, and she was right. I learned to solve problems easily on my own. I would plan out an outline before every project that I would begin in the future because of how much it made it easier for me on my Senior Project. I would also learn to ask for help whenever I can, and to learn from my mistakes.

The skills that I have obtained would be used in the future. Everything that I do will be based on the skills that I have discovered from my Senior Project, and will help me out enormously, whether I'm in college, or the service. It has made my life so much easier since I have learned these techniques. The skills that I have learned gave me the knowledge I would use later on in my life, and who knows where I will go now with the information.

I have discovered the one part of my life that I couldn't remember, the time when I was in the hospital. Before I started my Senior Project, I only remembered this one incident in the hospital bed, I was watching Star Wars on the television, and a large group of doctors walked into the room. They shut off the T.V. and asked me to lay on my stomach. I already knew what they were in there for, so I said no. They forced me onto my stomach, rolling me over into a pillow that was placed under my chest so my body was shaped into an arc. My father would hold my face down into the bed, almost suffocating me, as I did my best to try to set myself free, but I couldn't, I was too weak, and in too much pain. As I would calm down, they would inject a large needle into my spine, pumping the chemotherapy in and out with my spinal fluid so that it mixes well. This lasted 10 to 12 painful minutes. After the treatment, I would become very ill. The car rides home from Mass General Hospital in Boston would be a nightmare. I would throw up for the next 23 hours after my treatment, and I would become all puffy like a blowfish from the treatments.

Now I remember a little more of what happened to me when I was young. I remember what the doctors looked like. I remember the famous Dr. Truman, and how he saved my life. I remember my nurse, and how she sat by the bed the whole time holding my hand while the doctors were treating me with the chemotherapy. I remember how hard it was for my dad to see me the way I was and what his job was during this process. He said he hated being the bad guy, and he never wanted to hurt me, but he had to for the sake of my life. I have a better vision on how it used to be, and now that I remember a little more on how it was, I'm glad that I don't remember anything, I don't want to. I'm also happy that I got this at such a young age and I thank God that I had it at the age of three. It would be much harder on me and my family and friends if I had it when I am older; I am lucky.

I have learned to value life more now than I did before. I learned how hard it was for everyone to go through what I went through. I am so lucky for the help I was given through this whole process of my recovery and I can't thank my doctors, family, and friends enough for what they did for me. From my experience, I would love to help others out with the same problem that I had. Maybe that would be a career I could have in the future. I have always enjoyed helping others out, just like others helping me out. I respected the help that is given to me, and I would like to do it for others, all thanks to my experience due to this project. So I have learned a lot of values for myself, and plan to share them with everyone else.

The aspect that my Mission Statement reflects from my project is, don't be afraid to learn more about yourself than you already know. I have been surprised about my missing life, I never knew I was interviewed by *Time* magazine until I researched about myself, and I never knew that I was a famous leukemia patient. The doctors said that they had never seen a patient that was cured from Acute Lymphoblastic Leukemia 100% until they saw me, and how well my body handled the intense treatment of chemotherapy. I was totally shocked of the answers I have always wanted to know about myself. Even though my work on this project is done, my research will go on. I plan to get the whole story of my life, and find out where I end.

Lyz Trainor. Completing my Senior Project was the best thing I have ever done at Souhegan. At the beginning of the year I had to fight, beg, and plead to be a senior. I needed a lot of credits, I needed to focus, and I needed to do my Senior Project. It was looming over me like one big final test, the way for me to prove to everyone that it was a good idea for me to be a senior, and that I could do it. If I messed this up, I wouldn't live it down.

I took on this project with a lot of enthusiasm, but not without problems. I didn't have trouble picking my topic of nutrition. I figured there would be a lot of information and I could use the project to help me gain some more insight into my own stomach problems. I originally asked Susan Carr to be my mentor because she is a health teacher, but she already had two mentees. Not five minutes after Susan told me she couldn't be my mentor, Tom Sawyer walked by and I just asked him if he could do it. He agreed and I was on my way.

Looking back now, nothing about how I did this project surprises me. Even though I was caught off guard by the reaction I received to my presentation, the whole process was fairly typical of me. As I said before, I started this project with a lot of enthusiasm. I used the internet, went to the library and found an outside expert, a nutritionist/dietitian at St. Joseph's Hospital. I met with her twice and got a lot of information. So far everything was going great.

This carried me until around the second flag check, at which I got flagged. I had started to lose focus on my project. I was running into a lot of the same information and had lost touch with my expert. I didn't have a date to present and I just plain did not want to do this anymore. So I stopped. I stopped doing research, I stopped meeting with Tom, and I stopped caring. No big deal, I thought, I'll just present in May or June or whenever. My grades from first trimester were awful and my last progress report threatened the same thing for second trimester. I needed to concentrate on my regular classes and I thought that Senior Project was trivial.

So I continued not to worry until Regina Sullivan, my adviser, told me that I was to present on April 13th. I flipped out. I said there was no way I could do it, there must be some way out of it, etc. Again, a typical Lyz reaction. But after Regina sat me down and explained that there was no other option, I buckled down. I refocused my project more on dieting so I could get more information. Instead of going back to my expert, I went to a personal trainer so I could get more information on losing weight. As usual, the pressure was on. I was doing great. Sure, my stress level was through the roof and I was convinced I couldn't do it. I cursed the whole idea of Senior Project so often I didn't even realize how much information I was taking into my brain. I was so scared of the actual presentation, I couldn't talk. I turned into an absolute monster. I hated every minute of it. I kept thinking all this work for a 20-minute presentation. Then that would remind me that my presentation was only 13-minutes long, and I would freak out all over again.

During this whole thing, I often thought about my Division One Presentation. I went through the exact same cycle: started off with enthusiasm, somewhere in the middle deciding it was stupid and stopping, then pulling it all together in the last week. Even two years ago I was surprised at how my presentation went and ended up crying in Peggy Silva's arms after it was all over. And Senior Project was the exact same thing right down to the whole Peggy part. I also do this with small projects as well. It is just the way I have always done things.

Why do I put myself through it? I honestly do not know. Every time I set out to do something I tell myself I'm not going to give up or let things go till the last minute, but I always do and generally it works out for me. I did learn a lot about my topic. I was able to field questions afterwards and feel confident I could present again or talk about my topic in any setting. I was stressed out and miserable, but I brought it on myself. If I had to do this project again, I can almost guarantee I would do the same thing. This is the way I learn. It's probably not the best way and maybe some day I'll realize that and try something else. But for now, I think it's fine.

We were told to tie the Mission Statement and I can't. For the 4 years I have been at Souhegan, the only time I have heard the Mission Statement was when I was in trouble. It has just been something to turn around and kick me in the butt, not something I associate with good experiences. I could tell you that I pushed my comfortable limits and expanded my horizons, but I don't feel that way. I didn't think about the Mission Statement during the whole process. I did learn, though—I think that is apparent.

CHAPTER 5

Building and Sustaining a Strong Professional Culture

Studies of change efforts have found that the fate of new programs and ideas rests on teachers' and administrators' opportunities to learn, experiment, and adapt ideas to the local context. (Darling-Hammond, 1997, p. 214)

Some of the most exciting work we undertook at Souhegan was in response to our questioning the belief systems about how educators can and should work together. Rather than seeing ourselves as a scattered group of autonomous teachers and administrators, we challenged one another to create a true professional learning community. Although there is now a significant body of research to support the decisions we made in 1991, there was little firsthand experience available at that time. We felt intuitively that a powerful synergy could result from working together rather than separately, that the whole of what we could accomplish as a collective faculty would be much greater than the sum of our individual efforts.

Ironically, since 1991 much educational research has emerged to support our work. Most notably, Judith Warren Little and Milbrey McLaughlin (1993) of Stanford University reported on a 3-year study of effective schools and found that teachers most involved with examining their practices and pedagogy were members of strong collegial communities. "Not one teacher who had evolved this form of pedagogy and conception of classrooms was an isolate" (p. 97).

This concept of collaborative work is reinforced in other research undertaken in the 1990s. Some of the most significant work has been done at the Center on Organization and Restructuring of Schools at the University of Wisconsin. In a report on their research, Sharon Kruse and Karen Seashore Louis (1995) identified five elements critical to the existence of strong professional communities: reflective dialogue, de-privatization of practice, collective focus on student learning, collaboration, and shared norms and values. (p. 2)

Finally, as a result of his studies at the University of Georgia, Glickman has argued strongly that educationally successful schools are ones that have consciously created communities of professionals working together toward a common vision of teaching and learning. In a summary of his findings about successful schools, Glickman (1993) captures that essence of Souhegan's efforts to become a successful learning community:

> Finding 1: Faculty in successful schools are less satisfied with regard to their teaching than are faculty in the less successful schools.
> Finding 2: Successful schools are places where faculty members supervise and guide one another, plan courses together, and work in coordination.
> Finding 3: In successful schools, faculty members are not treated as subordinates but instead are regarded as the colleagues of administrators and others involved in decisions and actions.
> Finding 4: Faculty members, administrators, and others in successful schools have established norms of collegiality for discussing and debating the big questions about how to constantly renew and improve the educational environment for all students.
> Finding 5: Successful schools seek, produce, and consume information, and they see educational renewal as a continuing process, not as an event. (p. 16)

He concludes by saying that "these findings tell us what has always been known. Successful schools are places where adults work collaboratively, without hierarchical status, to answer the critical question of how to educate students better." (p. 18)

In this chapter, we chronicle our efforts to establish a professional learning community characterized by a high degree of reflection and inquiry, of sustained collaboration, and of the deprivatizing of much of our professional work. Moreover, we discuss our attempts to embody a collective commitment to the learning of all students and to the shared norms and values that would ensure that this learning would occur.

THE SOUHEGAN BLUES

> You know that I teach English so I think I know how to speak it, but when I came to Souhegan, they told me I had to tweak it,
> I got the blues, Talkin' Souhegan blues,
> I need *community review*, got to talk to old Jen Mueller I got the blues.

I don't know that *protocol,* I can't have that conversation,
got to go see old Ted Hall I need *peer mediation*
I got the blues, Talkin' Souhegan Blues, Maybe Houlihan and Eric
Mann will make me a behavioral linguistic learning plan for these
blues

I wanted to relax in the library so I went and asked my *mentor,*
she said there ain't no library at Souhegan it's an *information center*
I got the blues, talkin' Souhegan Blues. We got to clear this up with
a *chalk talk* or at least a *consultancy* I want to be actively engaged in
my community but I got the blues.

To *piggy back* on that idea, I need a *Socratic seminar*
I can't *advocate authentic professional growth with my mind body and
heart* with these crazy blues, talkin' Souhegan blues.
My comfortable limits need to expand but I can't communicate effectively
if I can't even understand my own *CFG*
I'd like an *administrative fishbowl,* so I went to Jim Bosman to ask
He said you know my plate is full and I don't teach language I
teach math
How about a *Fist to five, a clearing, a descriptive review*
Cause I don't think we're adhering to *Coalition Principle Number Two*
But I need something to help me get rid of these
Complex thinking
Self-direct learning
Knowledgeable person
Skilled information processin'
Talkin' Souhegan BLUES

Teacher Steve Dreher captured the lingo perfectly as he sang to us at
the annual faculty retreat. Our first 2 work days each year are spent at a
local camp. We read, we plan, we play, we reconnect as friends and colleagues, and, always, we sing. The first song we sang together in August
1992 was a children's verse, "Inch by inch, row by row, gonna make this
garden grow. All it takes is a rake and a hoe and a piece of fertile ground."
Steve's song underscores how much we have changed since those first
innocent days. Our language reflects how deeply we have absorbed the
Souhegan gestalt.

We could not do the work we do without a strong professional culture; consequently, we offer our staff the same support and expect the same
level of engagement that we ask of our students. The habits of reflection
and analysis focus our attention on, and promote a culture of, excellence,
of constant attention to improving our work.

Throughout, we have set standards for our professional performance in the areas of planning and preparation, learning environment, instruction, and professional responsibilities. Developing standards for our work, according to guidance counselor Carol Kreick, "allowed us to define our role as educational leaders within the school. By defining our outcomes and expectations, we aligned our work with our colleagues. This process grounded us because it offered a tool by which to measure our effectiveness in our work with students, parents, and colleagues."

As part of our Career Growth Plan, we invite teachers to choose an area of inquiry for 3 years and present their findings to their peers. Teachers who complete this work earn a $2,500 increase to their base salary.

"For all the obvious benefits of teacher leadership, there is also a caution," warns assistant superintendent Jennifer Fischer-Mueller:

> We offer many opportunities for teacher leadership in our school, but this requires a sense of balance. Too often, as our profession adopts new approaches to site-based management, reflective practice, or action research—all those things that classroom teachers can do to improve their schools—we do not provide the time or the reduced workload to accommodate these new and added responsibilities. It is essential that we help others to recognize that direct contact time with students needs to be supported by time to learn, time to reflect, time to collaborate with other professionals.

We have begun to address the need for sustained professional development time in varied ways. Once a month, students report to school 2 hours late, while our staff meets in Critical Friends Groups (CFGs), an initiative developed by the National School Reform Faculty (NSRF). Meeting in groups of eight to twelve, Critical Friends Groups seek to:

- Design learning goals for students, stated specifically enough that others can observe them in operation
- Design strategies that move students toward those goals
- Gather evidence on the effectiveness of those strategies
- Analyze and reflect upon that evidence
- Adapt teaching strategies and reformulate learning goals

Faculty members trained as coaches by the NSRF facilitate the monthly meetings, helping all professional staff to develop the skills of reflective practice.

As members of CFGs, we have learned how to talk to each other in honest, more critical ways, to give and request feedback on our work, to give support and to be pushed to think in different ways. By asking colleagues for help on improving curriculum and assessment strategies, we provide a window into each other's practice by making our work more public. We ask others to help us demonstrate that our work establishes high expectations for all students.

Each Critical Friends Group is comprised of a cross-section of professionals. A colleague presenting student work or asking for help with a professional dilemma discusses this work with English teachers, art teachers, music teachers, special educators, administrators, biology teachers, the school nurse, guidance counselors, and so forth. Each brings a unique perspective; the aggregate of their individual expertise strengthens the work by providing thoughtful discussion about the ways students learn.

We ask each member of a CFG to commit to their group for 2 years, knowing that it takes time for groups to work effectively with each other. In the fall of 2000, we invited our support staff to participate in their own CFGs, and the number of participants warrants dividing the group into two groups next year. In an ideal sense, we want all members of our professional community to seek feedback for their work and to help others improve their practice. If we are successful, the administrative role of evaluation and supervision should dovetail with the goals of our Critical Friends Groups.

Tenth-grade humanities teacher Aimee Gibbons discusses her experience in asking her Critical Friends Group to help her add authenticity and rigor to her work:

> In looking for a way to assess their reading beyond discussions aimed at finding the commonality of multiple texts, I asked students to use the theme of the book they read in developing a children's book, incorporating some specifics from their books in the story they wrote for children. I did not set any criteria for quality, and so I received stories that were very inappropriate for children; for example, a student who had read *The Color Purple* wrote a story about an orange that had been bruised and beaten up. It was wild.
>
> I asked my colleagues to "tune" the project sheet I had used for this unit. I asked them to look at the project sheet and asked them what they thought I was asking of my students. Their feedback helped me to establish a standard for the work and to include illustrations. Their questions helped me to establish more effective assessment criteria, and the quality of the stories improved, but I returned to my CFG with more questions. The questions my CFG asked kept leading me deeper into the work. They asked me to

consider questions of audience as my students developed their books, so I invited children in to listen to the stories. That upped the ante for my students, because if the little kids were not interested in the books, they started playing with other things or fidgeting. We discovered that an authentic audience made a difference to my student authors. They no longer had to please me; they had to please the real children listening to their stories.

I am still learning about this work. CFG colleague Kathy White suggested that her marketing students explore the possibility of finding a publisher for some of my students' stories. Her students developed a complete marketing plan, so next year she and I will collaborate on this work.

The perspective my CFG offers would be impossible for me to consider on my own. They think in different ways, and their attention to my work makes a difference. They focus on helping me answer my own questions about my work and my students' work.

Aimee refers to "tuning" her work—one of the protocols used in her CFG group. We believe that the use of formal protocols—guidelines for structuring the conversation—provide a safe environment for a teacher to ask for help and to be pushed in her thinking. These protocols provide tools for learning from students' work, for gaining perspective on a dilemma, for fine-tuning assessment systems, and for peer observation.

LEARNING FROM PROFESSIONAL PARTNERSHIPS

We were smart enough to know we needed help during our first few years. We invited other educators to serve as "critical friends" to our work, people who would help us to live our beliefs. Dr. Marcy Singer Gabella of Vanderbilt University helped to design our humanities framework before we opened the school; Dr. Tony Wagner mentored our first class of graduate interns from the University of New Hampshire and was our keynote speaker at a parents' forum early in our first year. Dr. Cheryl Jorgensen, the director of the Institute on Disabilities at the University of New Hampshire, helped train teachers to differentiate their instruction, to work with those students most challenged, and helped us build a culture of heterogeneity and inclusion.

Our membership in the Coalition of Essential Schools (CES) provided a set of 10 Common Principles to help us organize our beliefs; it also provided us with a strong professional association with others working in educational reform. The Coalition's annual conference gives us a chance to converse with others doing similar work. When we needed help in learning to work collaboratively, we asked CES associates Chris Louth and Stan Thompson to spend time with us consistently over 2 years to help our practice meet our promise.

Marilyn Wentworth, another CES colleague, offered us her expertise in learning how to communicate with each other. She studied our formal and informal structures and made suggestions that helped us to make more effective decisions. She taught us the art and skill of consensus-building.

We worked initially with the Annenberg Institute for School Reform over a 5-year period, and later with the National School Reform Faculty. They train our teachers to work together in a collaborative environment. To date, 12 of our staff have received training as Critical Friends Coaches, extending our professional development initiative.

We formed a critical friendship with Croton-Harmon High School in New York, traveling between the two schools a couple of times each year and meeting in the summer to obtain feedback on schoolwide initiatives. They supported our intent to do good work.

We were accepted into a 3-year research study with the RISER research group (Research in Secondary Education Reform, for youth with disabilities) at the University of Wisconsin. This group is studying the effects of secondary school reform on youths with disabilities. The data they collect during their visits will provide us with valuable information on educating all students.

We work closely with the University of New Hampshire to train graduate students entering the teaching profession, offering paid internships to students studying for their master's degree in education or teaching. These students, generally eight per year, spend the school year with us, teaching, coaching, advising extracurricular activities, mentoring Senior Projects, and serving as academic advisers. They gain experience in teaching in block schedules and working on interdisciplinary teams, and they participate in all professional development opportunities. Their professor, Eleanor Abrams, observes their work weekly and meets with them for a 2-hour seminar each week. Dr. Abrams believes:

> There is no better way to prepare people to teach than to teach. My students become reflective practitioners because it is an expectation of them in their formal studies and in their work here. There is a strong connection between the research on education and the work happening at Souhegan; it is a true learning laboratory. There is no substitute for this experience. The university relationship benefits both parties. Interns serve to lower the teacher/student ratio at Souhegan, and cooperating teachers become strong mentors to the interns.

We understand the work of training teachers new to the profession. We have also learned to rely on the valued expertise of our own education mentors. Public school educators work too often in isolation, trying to be all things to all people. By inviting the participation of external critical friends, we ask our peers to commit to our success. We ask them to walk in our shoes for awhile and then pose questions that will lead us further into the work and, ultimately, will lead us to our own answers.

As we honor the traditions of our student population, we also establish adult traditions. These begin each year with a round of Up and Down the Mountain, a game that invites us to connect after a summer apart. We deliberately use large group games as a way of relaxing after a serious work session, recognizing the importance of silliness in sustaining the goodwill of a community.

Both Terrence Deal and Steven Covey, in their writings on healthy organizations, cite the importance of rituals and tradition in every culture. We have paid attention to the powerful role of tradition in the adult culture of our school; our most distinct ritual is our annual Viking Funeral.

THE VIKING FUNERAL

In nature, plants and animals must shed their skin before they can grow. Turtles, snakes, the leaves on the trees. We can learn from this, and so, today, I ask you to join me in the ritual of shedding. Spend a few quiet minutes thinking through the schoolyear we have just completed. Are there memories that you need to release? What are the things you carry, the things you need to let go of so that you can leave for the summer without harmful baggage?

When you have finished reflecting on your year, write your thoughts on the scrap of paper in front of you, and join me at the river. (John Dowd, Souhegan teacher)

We arrive at school a little later than usual on the day after the kids have left for the summer to empty the clutter from our rooms. At 10:00, we gather for our last Community Meeting. Sitting in a large circle in the cafeteria, we say goodbye to those leaving us, thank our graduate interns for their year with us, and take the time to honor those who have made a difference in our lives. For the next hour or so, the meeting takes on its own momentum as we share our stories from the year just completed. At the close of our meeting, John Dowd prepares us for the Viking Funeral.

As we walk down to the Souhegan River, we speak in whispers. We stand on the riverbank, swatting endless mosquitoes and black flies, as John puts sand in the bottom of the boat. The boat is different each year. Once John used an aluminum watermelon weighed down with sand; another time, Martha Rives fashioned a swan's head out of cardboard to put in the prow. About 18 inches long, the boat is wedged into the sand on the river-bank. One by one, faculty members crumple small pieces of paper and place them in the boat, some silent, others sharing their thoughts aloud, all the while discarding those burdens of the past 10 months.

> I remember the sacred silence . . . the hushed tones. . . . Sometimes we laughed as a teacher crushed the name of a meeting she no longer had to attend or a mean-spirited parent with whom she had battled . . . someone letting go of an innocent crush she had on a colleague. . . . We laughed the next year as she let him go again.
>
> The Viking Funeral is the place people say goodbye to us, choked with tears, relating special memories of special friends. One year several people had lost parents; Gary faced us, put his slip in the boat, and told us he was letting go of the grief he felt at losing his dad. Instead, he said, he would take joy in his father's presence in his life and all that his father had stood for. John showed us his jagged, blood-red scrawling of the word *cancer*, as he took back his life. As Sally crushed her memories of a particu-lar difficult student, he appeared on a bridge above us; the next year we moved our site to a more private location. Stacy threw her daily planner onto the pile—getting rid of others who controlled her time. Many of us have let go of fear and frustration. . . . Each year someone discards feelings of insecurity, of not being good enough or smart enough. . . . We have stated publicly that we were releasing anger, pain, rage, and sadness. We have used the occasion to mark the silly and the profound . . . it is our most sacred ritual. (Members of the Faculty)

Once all of us have added our written thoughts, John wades out to the center of the river, sets the papers on fire, and releases the boat to the water's gentle flow. We all stand silently, watching it meander downstream, and then walk back to the school. Our schoolyear has ended.

Toward the end of the first year of the high school, John Dowd, our outdoor adventure/wellness teacher, was asked to think about a ceremony to mark the end our first year. John recalls:

> As we met each other for the first time in August of 1992, we knew that we had to establish traditions that would sustain us. We knew that traditions were important, and we were excited to start our

own, especially those of us who had been places where there were traditions we didn't appreciate.

I wanted to make our ceremony dramatic, and I knew I wanted to use water and fire. I remembered that old Kirk Douglas movie that had a ceremony called a Viking Funeral, and it all just came together.

I have been pleasantly surprised by how much people have taken this ritual to heart. Each year, I wonder if it's going to bomb, but I am willing to take that risk. The most memorable ceremonies have been when people have had a hard time with something, or they have cried over stress that they have felt in their jobs. That is so healthy for us as a community—to make time, to make room. What we do here—in our community meetings, in our CFGs, and at the Viking Funeral—is make that space for each other. We say, through our actions, that what is going on with each of us is so important to us that we are going to stop everything else and listen to each other. I know that there is an incredible absence of judgment as we listen to each other in those ways.

When I stood in front of the entire faculty last year and showed them my paper with the word *cancer* written with such anger, I said, "Coping with my wife's illness, this is how I feel, and I hope it hasn't affected my work, or the kids." Having every colleague witness my emotion took an incredible weight off my shoulders because now, everybody knew.

For Gary Schnakenberg, the design of the Viking Funeral set it apart from other traditions:

We had to create our own rituals. I had never really done that, although I had experienced an amalgamation of rituals. When families meld, they form traditions that retain pieces of the individual. Here it wasn't possible to incorporate individual experiences because we had come from so many different places. I have taken advantage of the Viking Funeral to say something to those who know something about me and to mark important occasions. It put words on the experience of losing my dad, and I wanted to let people who cared about me to know how I was thinking about that loss now. And when I said goodbye to Jo Ferrell, my world studies partner, I acknowledged the pain of that loss.

Tonya Bakewell Dreher had been hired to teach at Souhegan on the day of the Viking Funeral and was invited to attend our closing ceremony. She remembers

. . . being overwhelmed and not sure if it was real. I couldn't believe there was actually a place where teachers could admit that they had made mistakes, had let someone down, had falsely judged, had felt insecure. . . . These weren't the only things burned that day, but they impacted me the most. I had just finished a year at a school where no one ever asked how I was doing or if I needed anything. It had been a difficult time for me, and nobody knew or cared. It was as if there were a "don't ask, don't tell" attitude, and asking for help or admitting to having a problem was a definite sign of weakness. Inherently, I knew that schools should not be that way, but I'd never experienced another way. I knew that in order to be an effective teacher, I needed to be real and honest with myself and those around me. Most of all, I needed to know that others were experiencing the same things and having the same doubts and struggles at times.

    I watched and listened as my soon-to-be colleagues bared their souls and tossed a piece of paper onto the burning boat. The symbolism was powerful, and as we walked away, the group seemed more lighthearted.

Ted Hall burned his rookie mistakes as principal at the end of his first year in that job. He expressed regret at eliciting powerful negative feelings as he wended his way through a difficult personnel issue. As he placed his crumpled paper in the boat, he let go of the necessary experience of being new in his job.

    Using the archetypes of fire and water to gather us at the river at the end of our year, John Dowd taps into our need to express our humanity, to laugh and cry together, to connect the strands of our individual lives. And when we turn to each other and acknowledge our struggles, we begin to recognize that we do not need to wait for the river. We learn to reach out to each other; we learn, as Tonya Bakewell Dreher says, to "grow as a teacher and a person, to let go of being suspicious when people express an interest in my teaching, my practice, my curriculum, and my life." We learn to accept each other as sincere members of a learning community.

MENTORING AND SUSTAINING NEW STAFF

    Several years ago, we began to pay close attention to how we welcome new teachers, knowing how difficult it is to enter a strong professional culture. In addition to attending our annual 2-day retreat, we ask new teachers and interns to attend a 3-day orientation. We also assign each new teacher a mentor who serves as a formal resource to the newcomer. We have begun a newcomers' Critical Friends Group so that this group can learn the tools we use to improve student achievement, providing a stable environment in which to build collegial ties.

Despite our attention to the needs of newcomers, we have discovered that rapid growth is impacting our ability to ensure that their transition to Souhegan is a smooth one. Last year we added 17 new teachers, a record number. Some new hires filled new positions; others replaced teachers who left the school. Interviews with a cross-section of new hires reveals that we still have work to do in this area. During the spring of their first year at Souhegan, we asked them to talk about their decision to teach here and to relate some of their experiences during their first year at the school.

George Darden found our Web site, (www.sprise.com/SHS) in the middle of June, after finishing a master's program at the University of Michigan. George wanted to take a big risk and explore a different region of the country from his native Georgia. He joined a ninth-grade team as a social studies teacher.

Dr. Kathleen Pierce knew about the work of the Coalition of Essential Schools and had subscribed to its publication, *Horace,* for many years.

Jane Flythe was recruited from a neighboring school district to join our special education department. Jane's son is a tenth-grade student at Souhegan.

Kathleen Desmond's own high school principal was Dr. Bob Mackin, who left after her graduation to open Souhegan High School. When she later moved from New York to New Hampshire, she worked for several years in another district before joining our modern language department as a Spanish teacher.

GEORGE: I was extremely conscious of entering a "community of learners, born of respect, trust, and courage." The notion of community gives you a sense of doing something bigger than you could as an individual. I felt on the fringe, though, wondering what my ticket was to get into this community. I struggled to find my niche. My team provides support, but I am impatient to feel a sense of belonging.

JANE: I have felt impatient also. As an experienced special educator, I have stuff to share and I know that the school wants my expertise because they hired me. It has been difficult to figure out how to enter the conversation, especially in a place where professional relationships are already firmly established. This school has very confident teachers, and sometimes it is hard to find a way in.

KATHLEEN PIERCE: I have not known what to do with my little bags of tricks of knowledge and enthusiasm. As a teacher with 18 years of experience, I want to feel like my presence makes a difference.

KATHLEEN DESMOND: My experience has been so different. I have made solid professional friendships. Jolene Sawyer and I plan our work together and have developed some great ideas. In terms of the greater school entity, I chose to sit back and observe. I deliberately chose to wait until my first year here was completed before taking on schoolwide work. If anything, I held back from forming immediate friendships because of a past professional experience when I jumped too quickly into friendships that caused me some problems later.

GEORGE: Although I have questions about forging adult relationships, I have completely enjoyed my relationship with students. Kids here enjoy positive relationships with adults, and those relationships are enhanced, I think, by the fact that our students call us by our first names. Coaching the track team also helps me know many more students than the ones on my team.

KATHLEEN PIERCE: George has a significant advantage. As a member of a ninth-grade team, I only see my team. I do not have a sense of the whole school. This can lead to that sense of "team tunnel vision" that George has spoken about.

KATHLEEN DESMOND: I am not on a team, so I sometimes do feel left out. During the recent tenth-grade testing, my schedule was interrupted routinely, but the teams were not aware of this. Testing was stressful for all tenth-grade teachers, though, on-team and off.

Although I understand all the variables involved in including off-team teachers in parent meetings, I miss the opportunity to meet some of the parents of my students. Being off-team, however, gives me the opportunity to teach different grades of students. I like that mix. Teachers on-team don't have that advantage.

GEORGE: For me, the benefit of working only with one age group is the developmental knowledge I have of the age group I teach. I never considered, however, that in order for me to be more included, nonteam teachers are excluded—forced out of some conversations. I don't know how to solve for that. I never even thought about that as a problem.

KATHLEEN PIERCE: This educational community was built around the idea of changing the status quo. There is justifiable pride in what was accomplished. I wonder whether there is room for good ideas now that it is an institution with a sense of status quo. I also have wondered about how the school acts on its values. For instance, if interdisciplinary work is valued, is there a standard of expectations around that value?

GEORGE: As a first-year teacher, I would have had difficulty with that as a standard. I am too busy trying to think through my own work to accommodate another voice. Sometimes, this is a logistical problem. What I have most benefited from at Souhegan is the appreciation for the artistry of teaching. I feel supported as an artist because the things I do are very specific to me. The way I teach reflects my personality; my ninth-grade colleagues and I are responsible for the same content and skills, but we deliver them very differently. My team is doing some interdisciplinary work together, a skills-based unit that involves all of us. I could not have done this work until now, at the end of the school year.

KATHLEEN PIERCE: I, too, appreciate that sense of artistry that my work encourages, but I expected to work in an interdisciplinary setting, and that didn't work out this year. I look forward to the collaborative potential of CFG, to have colleagues who will come into my classroom and observe my work.

JANE: Yes, CFG is a very democratic group. I enjoy the atmosphere, the sense of getting to know a group of colleagues, and sharing our experiences. Those conversations have been important to me.

GEORGE: CFGs and Advisories are the two best innovations of the school. I wish CFG could be more embedded into the culture, not limited to monthly 2-hour meetings. I also wish the school offered more social gatherings. I am not suggesting that the school engineer my social life, but it has been difficult to get to know people.

KATHLEEN DESMOND: I know what you mean, George. The people I know best are probably the 17 newcomers in my CFG. I have enjoyed that group a lot.

JANE: You know, our conversation isn't too different from the conversations I had with my son Jonathan when he transferred to Souhegan. My strongest endorsement of the school is that I entrust these people with Jonathan, but when he was the new kid on the block, he had to figure out who would become his friends, who he had stuff in common with, who could help him. It was much easier for me to be the sage on the sidelines giving him advice.

Kathleen Desmond's comment about 17 new teachers in 1 year is telling as to why there is a feeling of disenfranchisement among some new members of the faculty. As children often ask the waves to stop until they can get into the water, so, too, we wish we could stave off our tsunami of growth until we find a way to recapture the ingredients that most welcome new voices and new ideas. It is ironic that a school founded on new ideas is perceived by some as blocking new ideas. We wonder whether the thoughts expressed are particular to Souhegan, or whether every situation requires its own season of newness.

As a special educator, Jane Flythe expected collegial partnerships with other teachers, only to find that students perceived her as an assistant to the classroom teachers. Is team-teaching a realistic goal for new pairings of strangers, or is every new experience particular to a specific group of individuals? Kathleen Pierce expected that interdisciplinary work would be the norm on her team. Do new teams need time to get to know each other, or should they get to know each other through sharing their work? We give teams common planning times and a common set of students and believe that they will find a way to connect their work, but we stop short at mandating those connections. Would an immediate culture of shared work have helped George or hindered his development as a first-year teacher? What is the proper balance between the "one-room schoolhouse" model of isolated teaching and an interdisciplinary environment? What is our responsibility to provide social encounters for our staff? Could it be that our very emphasis on the concept of community establishes a set of social expectations beyond that of a collegial work environment? If so, are those expectations valid? We have many questions.

Kathleen Desmond and Jane Flythe are staying at Souhegan. Kathleen Pierce has also chosen to stay and will teach two senior seminars next year. Both Jane and Kathleen will have, in effect, another first year as they begin relationships with new teaching partners. It will be interesting to ask again for their impressions as they continue their work at Souhegan. George Darden initially thought that he would stay at Souhegan for 4 years before returning to his Georgia roots, but the lack of social connections caused him to leave at the end of his first year. He says, "There are 159 counties in Georgia and I know every single one of them. There is something to be said for that."

CHAPTER 6

The Change
Process Continues

A leader focuses not on [his] own image as leader, but on the tone of the body
of the institution. Followers, not leaders, accomplish the work of the organization. We need to be concerned, therefore, with how the followers deal with
change. (DePree, 1992, p. 28)

The history of education reform at the high school level is littered with
examples of redesigned schools that collapse once a strong leader departs.
As I (Bob) prepared to leave Souhegan in 1998, I was determined not to see
the school become another casualty of short-lived innovative thinking. Rather
than allowing my departure to signal the end of an era, I worked to ensure
that Souhegan continue in an image that reflected more than my personality.

Having served as principal on previous occasions, I recognized the
necessity of planning well in advance for leadership transition. The first
section of this chapter is my story. Then Ted Hall, my successor, shares his
perspective on transition. He goes on to speak with great candor and poi-
gnancy about the challenge of leadership for a rookie principal, com-
pounded by the new pressures of population growth and the resulting
space squeeze. This discussion of the impact of sheer size on maintaining
a personalized school—the heart of the challenge facing Souhegan in the
years ahead—brings the chapter to a close.

We end our writing with Peggy's model of the change process and my
summary of lessons learned from the Souhegan experience.

TRANSITIONAL LEADERSHIP

Bob Mackin, Principal, 1991–1998

Historically, democracies survive their leaders. The smooth transition
of leadership is embedded into democratic cultures, where, unlike in many

other forms of governance, no single individual or governing elite "owns" the culture. The very nature of democracy assumes shared norms and values and a dissemination of authority. For Souhegan to be a successful democratic school, therefore, it was necessary to create shared stakeholders from the outset, to decentralize the leadership of the organization. Singular authority is nonsustainable; an organization that rests on the charisma and ego of one leader seldom survives that leader's exit. Therefore, transferring and decentralizing authority becomes an essential task of effective leadership.

One traditional means of creating a democratic culture is reflected in an organization's formal structures and the ways in which it defines personnel roles. In our case, we consciously created a broad cadre of teacher leaders. We gave stipends to teachers who served as the six captains of teams in grades 9 and 10, and teachers who facilitated the work of Senior Project, the Division One Exhibition, and Advisory. We met with these individuals regularly, providing guidance, support, and, most importantly, access. We pushed decision making as far down the organization chart as possible, recognizing that our model of continuous conversation would ensure that decisions would be in concert with our mission. This conscious effort to empower a broad range of individuals allowed us to grow our future school leaders. At the same time it provided assurance that the institutionalization of key values, principles, and practices would occur, which in turn would transcend the influence of any single leader.

In spite of the best efforts of teachers to embed the culture of the school with a set of institutionalized values and practices, a misdirected principal can wreak havoc on a school's mission and direction. Even the strongest school culture may not be able to survive a principal who seeks to dismantle key elements of the organization. Although I stayed for 2 years longer than the 5 I had originally promised, I knew from the outset that I needed to provide a smooth transition of leadership that would enhance the chances that Souhegan would be sustained as we had envisioned it. I also knew that there was a national vacuum of individuals who could lead an initiative that was as uniquely mission-driven as Souhegan.

When I first met Ted Hall, I knew that he had the mindset and the ability to lead a school such as ours. I literally met him on a bus in Chicago, during a Coalition of Essential School's function. He was an assistant principal at Catalina Foothills High School, in Tucson, Arizona, a school that opened at the same time as Souhegan. Ted had reluctantly stepped into the role of interim principal of that school 3 months into its first year after its founding principal left. We established a link then of shared experiences, and we kept in touch when he left Tucson to accept a position with the Coalition of Essential Schools, then located at Brown University. We had had a series of turnovers in our dean of students' position and were delighted when Ted successfully interviewed for that position in the spring of 1996. While I recognized Ted's potential and clearly saw him as a prospective successor, he obviously would need to prove himself to a broader audience, to earn the respect of students, parents, support staff, and faculty. Fortunately he was able to do just that.

The transference of leadership requires transparent facilitation. Future leaders must know and understand the organization's stories, and they must model positive behaviors that align with the school's mission. They must be an integral part of the teaching and learning that happens in every corner of a school, as observers and as participants. They must reflect on their own learning, and they must display the disposition to foster strong relationships with the many constituencies of a school community. An established leader must become a strong mentor to all those members of the school community who will remain within the organization. In essence, he or she must ensure that the loss of their role as vision-keeper, as the symbolic head of the family, is addressed consciously by the school as a whole and that the protection of the vision becomes the role of everyone within the organization. In this respect, the role of the larger faculty becomes significant. They must assume a major responsibility for mentoring the new leader as well. The assumption must be that every individual is fully responsible for the overall integrity and mission of the school.

Before I chose to leave, Souhegan had completed its initial accreditation with the New England Association for Schools and Colleges (NEASC) and had met most of its initial challenges. I felt that a shift in leadership would be healthy and timely. Ted Hall was clearly ready to lead the school. A national search affirmed our belief that Ted not only had the skills to maintain the vision and the key practices of the organization but also was head and shoulders above the other candidates who applied for the position.

Ted Hall, Principal, 1998–Present

My second year as dean of students, 1998, was a year of great transition. The staff had begun to grieve Bob's decision to leave. Allison Rowe, our dean of faculty, retired that year, and Jennifer Fischer-Mueller took Allison's job. Shortly after I was selected as principal, we added another dean of faculty, Jim Bosman, and hired Ted Houlihan to replace me as the dean of students.

The four new administrators took the reins of a different school than had opened in 1992, a school still pledged to the Coalition principles and a strong sense of mission, but no longer a start-up venture. We were a social institution with a history—and many emerging needs as well.

While working at the Coalition of Essential Schools, Ted Sizer, the founder of this organization, told me that the best preparation for the work we were all trying to do would be to go and spend time working for Rick Lalley and Bob Mackin at Souhegan High School. Bob and I had established a strong collegial relationship by that point. He had in fact asked me to apply for the dean of student's job, in 1994, just after I had committed to the Coalition. When this job became available again in 1996, I applied. Bob told me that he planned to step down as principal in a year or two, and although he could not guarantee me the position as his successor, he did tell me that I would have the opportunity to demonstrate my readiness.

Bob understood the responsibilities of transition. He made sure that I was involved in every aspect of decision making, but it was a tragedy at school that triggered the true start of the formal transition of leadership. Bob had just arrived in Atlanta for a conference when I called to tell him that a student had died. While he made plans to return to New Hampshire, I gathered teachers, counselors, and students together to plan a memorial service for this student at school. When Bob returned, we worked together to help the community deal with this crisis. While Bob's immediate return from his trip made a symbolic difference to all of us, the school community knew that we had taken good care of everyone in his absence.

Graduation that year also served as a transition. Bob was extremely gracious in his introduction of me as the new principal of Souhegan. This was indicative of a key ingredient in our shift in leadership. Nothing about Bob was ever about his "ownership" of the school; everything was about maintaining the integrity of the work. He and Allison had laid a solid groundwork for others to continue the hard work of sustaining a very different school like Souhegan. From the inception of the school, they defined their work as helping others to succeed. Ego was never a factor.

One of the first things I did as principal was to hold interviews with each adult member of the school. They did not reveal a need to change course; the only nervousness people expressed was about life without Bob Mackin. That was particularly true for teachers who had started their careers with Bob as their first principal. It was also true for a few charter faculty members who did not know how the transition of leadership would affect their job satisfaction. Some of the students also wondered whether I could shake the mantle of dean of students as I began work requiring a shift in perspective.

Bob and I have very different personalities, so I knew that others would not expect me to be his clone. I did know, though, that we would continue to rely on the Mission Statement and the vision that had served the school well for its first 6 years.

In many ways, I am not the principal of the same school that hired me, as we have added more than 150 students in just 2 years. The school is different because we have many more staff members; it is different because we have many more students; it is different because we have reached a critical mass of both of those with regard to our ability to personalize. The biggest question facing us is how to retain our commitment to our core values in a school that has almost doubled in size since it opened in 1992. This issue affects every program and policy in the school. Regardless of all the other aspects of being principal, this issue will define my leadership of the school.

The weight of growth is threatening the support beams in place. To preserve the foundation, we need to design different supports. Instead of a school of 900 or 1,000 or 1,200, we need to reduce the scale—to find organizational structures that will ensure that we continue to know every student well.

Rapid growth has made the distinctions between Division One and Division Two more striking. Division One continues to be a place where kids are nurtured. While we have more teams, the size of the teams has not changed. Moreover, the teams have figured out what you do to maintain a personalized environment, and they continue to honor that. Their work has only gotten better in terms of communication with parents, students, guidance counselors, and so forth. They use the results from the Division One Exhibition to improve their work with students. Because of the insularity of teams, the members are able to pass along the cultural norms of Souhegan to new colleagues.

At Division Two, we now have 200+ students in each grade, and without teams we do not have as much individual knowledge of these students. A teacher hired for a position at Division Two has a greater likelihood of retaining old habits because there is less formal attention paid to acculturation—and that becomes its own form of acculturation, of course.

We have all lost a small-school experience, and we are still grieving that loss. In a place that values community, how do we maintain small-school values in a time of rampant growth?

Thinking about dividing the school into some form of smaller units causes its own tensions. Debbie Meier, currently principal of the Mission Hill School in Roxbury, Massachusetts, believes that the ideal staff for a school is the number that can sit around a conference table. At Souhegan, we are still trying to have community meetings for a circle of 95 people. We haven't been able to develop new strategies for dealing with twice as many people. We have so many questions, and no time to play with possible answers. The initial planning team of the high school had a year to consider the possibilities of forming new structures; we have to do it in real time, between progress reports and the prom.

Our next innovation should not be solely one of structural changes, and yet I also feel a sense of compelling urgency to resolve structural direction. The tension is that specialization occurs with size. How do we avoid the bureaucracy that comes with size, the sense that there are as many adults performing jobs that occur outside the classroom as there are adults present in the classroom? Democracy is a messy process; consensus traditionally favors the status quo. At what point do we simply charge forward?

A simple example of charging forward occurred recently with our decision to use one style of narrative progress reports for both Division One and Division Two. The final product was wildly successful—the new progress reports had a huge positive impact on our parents—but making that shift in reporting caused a great deal of anxiety for some teachers. The balance between supporting change and executing change is difficult to achieve.

Another simple example of change occurred for me after a chance question from another principal. Her casual question about how often I met with our teaching teams forced me to recognize that I never met with them. Team captains met routinely with the dean of faculty, but I never sat down and listened to one of their team meetings. Now I do, and it's great. I love the banter of groups that know each other well, and I have a much broader picture of the life of our school. The teams appreciate my presence.

Last year, we decided to consolidate Senior Project presentations into a single week, instead of staggering them over several weeks. We asked for input, and despite some expressed nervousness, we went ahead with the idea. Looking back and assessing the positive responses to the changes, I learned again the value of making decisions that move the work forward.

I struggle with how to get to the next level of professional development, aligning our Learner Expectations with our graduation requirements. Establishing competencies for each course would give us so much vertical and horizontal knowledge about our students. For instance, our ninth-grade students all take part in a very powerful initial science unit, the rocket launch. The three ninth-grade science teachers have done excellent work in producing authentic curriculum and assessments. They learn an incredible amount of information about each of their students. The next step would be to use this assessment to gain a common understanding of the knowledge and skills gained by the whole. I know that we could learn a lot about the necessary next steps in improving student learning from common assessments across grade levels.

My biggest challenge at this time is to establish the framework and timetable for the changes that need to occur. There is danger in delaying this work. We have already seen the incremental changes to programs necessitated by growth. Our ninth-grade students have to eat lunch at 10:30 in the morning to accommodate the numbers of students in the cafeteria at any one time. We have had to adjust schedules and room assignments, and those changes affect curriculum. The change is subtle, but it represents a shift in our focus.

My role as the principal is to notice and question each change, to ask whether the change has a positive or negative effect on our mission. My work is analogous to that of a gardener; gardeners prune the little branches that spring from the bottom of trees in order for the trees to remain strong. Strong trees have strong branches that connect to the trunk. As principal, I must be aware of the shape and strength of our school, encourage ideas that generate from the core and strengthen our roots, and prune that which threatens the future health and strength of our school.

My involvement in the core practices of the school will continue to help me to be a better principal. As an adviser to 10 seniors, my job is to shepherd them through their Senior Projects, as well as serving as a mentor to two seniors. As I constantly juggle my schedule to accommodate the needs of my students, I understand the work on a much deeper level. I have a much deeper awareness of the depth and breadth of the work because I am a participant in the work. As an adviser and as the school principal, I appreciate the clear articulation of student accountability. Every single student understands the boundaries of Senior Project. They each receive a tremendous amount of support to help each of them reach our very high expectations for their achievements.

I am still learning my job. As a third-year principal, I am still a rookie in many ways. I have begun to think more about the whole, not just the pieces, of each day's work. Strategies that enhance teaching, learning, curriculum, and assessment require me to spend more time in classrooms with teachers and provide more support to academic coordinators. A more sustained focus on student progress in our Learner Expectations will help teachers in their work.

I have more questions than I do answers. How do we sustain staff autonomy without sacrificing the shared expectations of our learning community? How can we strengthen and sustain our democratic governance? How can we communicate effectively with more than 100 adults? Are the same rituals effective in a population that has doubled? How can we encourage teachers to move from Division Two to Division One? How do we help teams? How can we help teachers to be more effective practitioners? My questions exhaust me.

I don't think personalization is a function of size, but I do think that it is affected by rapid changes in size. Small things change, causing shifts in future expectations. For example, fewer teachers dressed up for Halloween this year, a small thing. A small, insignificant change, but is that an indicator of cultural shift?

If I have a chance to see most teachers every day, then they will tell me if they plan to miss a meeting or must arrive late. If I do not see them routinely, there is less of a tendency to provide that courtesy. Projecting this idea forward, I wonder if larger organizations require more traditional forms of accountability?

It is not by chance that the words I speak most frequently are *struggle*, *tension, balance*, and *growth*. Reflective practice needs space—physical space and time, and emotional space from daily events—and we are all impacted by the current lack of space in our school in many ways. The work is worthwhile, but never easy.

The one constant remains my pride in our students. I love hanging out with our kids. I love being stopped in the hallway by a student eager to have me read her letter to her roundtable for her Division One Exhibition. I love that kids want teachers and administrators to attend their prom; we are doing something right when students include us in their lives. I love bringing my own young sons to school and watching the high school kids reach out to them. I love knowing that visitors see intense student engagement as they visit classrooms and talk to students in the halls. I love to see kids' pride as they stand in front of their peers and their teachers and speak with great authority.

As an adviser, a Senior Project mentor, a facilitator of one of our Critical Friends Groups, and principal, I am proud of our work. We are at a turning point in terms of size, but we understand the complexities of sustaining an effective learning community, and every day we respond to our students' needs and desires. That is a strong achievement.

MANAGING CHANGE ONCE AGAIN

This heading assumes good intentions. More appropriate titles might be "Wallowing in Change," "Barely Surviving Change," "Drowning in Change"—you get the idea. The truth is that right now change is managing us. We painstakingly planned programs and policies for a school of 800, a school that would not require an addition until the year 2008. As I (Peggy) write this chapter in the spring of 2001, we have 970 students. We expect to register another 30 or so this summer, and we have added two more portable classrooms to the six we already have.

We have begun to wonder how personalization can happen with so many persons, how we can operate in a humane manner with so many humans. We can offer many indicators of stress on the adult and student culture of the school—fewer social gatherings for faculty, lower rates of attendance at meetings, more litter in the hallway, fewer kids vying for seats on the Community Council, and so forth. Ironically, as we add more people, we add more separation between people. Marketing teacher Kathy White points to a business axiom called the Rule of 20s—for every 20 feet of physical space separating individuals, there is an increased gap in communication. We are addressing the need for physical space with plans for an additional building on our campus, but we have begun to question the need for systemic changes in our programs and structures as well.

We have a sense that we do not invoke the Mission Statement as frequently in our daily work. In some intangible ways, the school feels less centered, a bit adrift. It is easy to point to the lack of space as one stressor, but people wonder whether the school culture is subtly shifting away from its practice of democratic principles. Principal Ted Hall wonders whether larger schools drift unconsciously toward more authoritative structures—whether it is easier to engage an active citizenry when everyone knows everyone else and interacts regularly. He believes that it is difficult to ensure that all opinions have been aired in meetings of one hundred participants.

In the spring of 2000, Souhegan applied for a grant from the New Hampshire Department of Education. This grant would provide the opportunity for 14 members of the Souhegan community to attend a week-long retreat in July as part of the Best Schools' Initiative. To prepare for this work, Ted Hall convened a "think tank" of interested faculty and school board members for a 2-day off-site retreat. His intent was to examine in great depth the need for restructuring. Using the Mission Statement as a focus, Ted asked the group to think anew about the ideal environment for students. Participants explored different concepts of space, time, and program: One group focused on whether Souhegan's Learner Expectations were achievable goals for all students in our school of inclusion; another explored moving the boundaries of school to include internships and travel/study opportunities; another discussed the feasibility of redesigning the schoolday. These brainstorming sessions laid the groundwork for the team who would spend a week during the summer further developing long-term goals.

In addition to studying the ideas initiated by members of the earlier group, Souhegan's Best Schools' team reviewed goals established by the Souhegan School Board; recommendations of the New England Association of Schools and Colleges (NEASC), our accrediting organization; data from Souhegan's performance on the New Hampshire State Assessment test; and the end-of-year staff survey. They also studied Souhegan's founding documents: the 10 Common Principles of the Coalition of Essential Schools, the Mission Statement, the Souhegan Six, and Souhegan's Learner Expectations. Finally, they examined samples of student work from the Division One Exhibition, Junior Research Papers, and Senior Projects. Their mission was to define long-term goals for the high school, establish topics for further study, and develop a timeline for each goal. When school reopened in September, Ted Hall would call for volunteers to serve on a steering committee to coordinate this work.

The four goals developed by this team were:

1. To meet the needs of all students
2. To strengthen the personalization of our teaching and learning environment
3. To use a common language in assessing and reporting student learning
4. To strengthen democratic practices that involve all who are directly affected by the school

Ted's plan to establish a steering committee when school opened was derailed by a shift in the school's administration. One of our deans of faculty, Jennifer Fischer-Mueller, became our district's assistant superintendent. Allison Rowe, Souhegan's original dean of faculty, returned to serve as an interim administrator. Although Ted did make a presentation to the faculty about the work of the Best Schools' team, he did not appoint the steering committee.

Over the next few months, the faculty engaged in several discussions about possible ways to reduce the scale of the school. Their conversations focused on ways in which the school could strengthen personalization in light of a student body that would grow to a projected size of 1,200 students within the next 5 years. They discussed the idea of assigning staff and students to one of three smaller units, or houses, within the existing school. During these discussions, the administration and faculty came to realize that they did not share a common vision of structures that would provide further personalization, although all agreed with guidance counselor Brian Irwin's reminder that every conversation regarding change had to stem from the Mission Statement.

Social studies teacher Marcey Rawitscher stated that it was "difficult to think outside the box if you are already in a box." Eric Mann noted that the suggestion to move to three smaller units was actually a request that we function more effectively as a larger unit. His thought was that, as we have grown, "we have all retreated to smaller subsets of 'belonging'— teams, departments, lunch-table friends, and so forth. The suggestion to divide the school into three smaller entities would once again ask us to be accountable for a larger circle."

Principal Ted Hall recognizes his dilemma.

We all know that we have to move forward, that we need to strengthen our sense of community. At the same time, the need to change produces fear, anxiety, and uncertainty. We all feel frustrated. Compounding this is our need to replace both deans of faculty; Jennifer became assistant superintendent in the fall and Jim Bosman has decided to return to teaching math full-time next fall. I need to form a steering committee and I need to run the school at the same time.

Glancing at the clock, Ted chuckled, adding that he also had to make the daily announcements. At 7:30 A.M., it was the start of another schoolday.

Ted wants to move forward. He worries that without a plan, we will stagnate. The staff worry that the onus of creating new administrative and educational structures will fall on their shoulders at the end of their workday. Other stakeholders—parents, students, the community, the school board, the superintendent—have not yet been included in the work. Without a steering committee, and without a clear, constant communication channel, the restructuring plan is stuck in place.

One explicit lesson we learned while planning Souhegan High School is that "thinking time" is essential. Unfortunately, in an active school environment, 1 year in school time translates into two 90-minute meetings each month, one devoted to existing initiatives, one devoted to the change process—a sum total of 900 minutes, or 15 hours. In contrast, the original planning team put in a full year of 12-hour days and then worked with the founding faculty and staff (mostly Type A personalities chosen specifically for their tolerance for ambiguity and chaos) for 3 weeks. Every decision, minuscule or mighty, made during that period was measured against the template of the Mission Statement. We were not distracted by Rent-a-Senior Day, flu season, graffiti on the music risers, plans for the semiformal, or the need to plan for the instruction and assessment of 970 teenagers. Mobilizing people to think about change is much more difficult when that work has to compete with other, immediate needs.

That we are stuck in place at the moment is not very troubling; it is an expected first step in a new change process. Michael Fullan (1993), writing about the complexity of change, notes that "under conditions of uncertainty, learning, anxiety, difficulties, and fear of the unknown are *intrinsic* . . . especially at the early stages" (p. 25, emphasis in original). What will support our prospective changes is that we have already established "the habits and skills required to engage in continuous corrective analysis and action" (Fullan, 1993, p. 5). Those habits and skills, articulated in our Mission Statement, remind us daily of who we want to be:

"We aspire to be a community of learners born of trust, respect, and courage." At the heart of the intense debate and inquiry that will inspire this change and self-renewal is our very strong model of professional development—a model that has provided us with the tools and collaborative skills to engage in difficult conversations about our work.

We understand the need "to challenge and expand the comfortable limits of thought, tolerance, and performance." We have demonstrated our ability to foster continuous change. We have restructured our administrative model several times to support our work; we designed and implemented the Division One Exhibition, knowing that our entire faculty would agree to participate in the roundtables for our tenth-grade students. We have participated in summer workshops to change curriculum in key academic disciplines.

We have encouraged teachers to develop new programs to improve and enhance student learning because the road map that is our Mission Statement directs us "to develop and empower the mind, body, and heart."

And, finally, the tension that is pushing us to reexamine our existing structures is the mandate "to support and engage an individual's unique gifts, passions, and interests."

Our deep spirit of inquiry plus our history of positive risk taking and the willingness to engage in extended messy conversations will lead us to the next essential ingredient of the change process, "positive contagion" (Fullan, 1993, p. 31).

Organization specialists caution that the change process is nonlinear. They draw reciprocal arrows between the data-gathering phase, the implementation phase, the monitoring and evaluation phase. The schematics accompanying each change model seem tidy—boxes and circles leading from left to right, up to down. The real-life survivor model of change, however, more closely resembles an old Nintendo video game, Super Mario Brothers.

Imagine the brothers navigating through a minefield, their little legs churning in constant motion. The brothers need to progress through a series of columns marked "planning," "implementation," "monitoring," and "evaluation." Before they can advance, they must touch every stakeholder and every tenet of the Mission Statement, earning points toward their goal. Each time they touch these bases, they must spend time on stations marked "communication," "reflection," and "revision." Further, they must take action against blobs of apathy, anxiety, and assorted menacing forces before proceeding. They must address the hurdles of "curriculum," "instruction," "assessment," and "personalization." They must focus on the next step, but constantly monitor and sometimes repeat all the steps already taken, all the time trying to beat the clock. As the game accelerates, the finish line sometimes seems tantalizingly close—but it moves every time the players get within reach. Constant noise accompanies the game, and shape-shifters cause chaos throughout.

This is the game of change. With one hand on the joystick of restructuring, we must keep the other hand juggling all the "stuff" of high school, the joys and challenges of leading an adolescent population through the riptides of their teenage years. It is arduous work.

THE LESSONS OF SOUHEGAN HIGH SCHOOL

We host many visitors to our school. We have met educators from Thailand, Israel, and Great Britain; we have spent our days with school superintendents, principals, school board members, and teachers from Maine to California. Their greatest question is how to begin and how to sustain a changed environment. As we respond, we recognize that we had the luxury of beginning with a new school, a new staff, and a commitment to change from our communities—a luxury not shared by many schools who wage tremendous external and internal battles in order to meet the needs of their students. Nevertheless, we have learned along the way that there are specific lessons in the act of creation, the process of change, and the fundamental human dynamics of schools as institutions.

1. *One person can unleash a torrent of change.* Superintendent Richard Lalley, a man of quiet fortitude and stoic vision, was able to transcend what had always been and dream of what could be. Out of his boldness came Souhegan High School.
2. *A community task force with a clear charge for its collective work and a willingness to learn together can set the stage for a very new vision.* A group of community members, as diverse as can be found in New Hampshire, became united in their commitment to read, to think, and to debate about a very different way to address the future of secondary schooling.
3. *The principal must ultimately be the vision-keeper.* I (Bob) brought a vision congruent with that of the community planning task force and the practical experience in making such a vision work. In quick time I became more than the principal—I was the vision-keeper.
4. *Schools can and must be mission-driven.* The common purpose shared by the planning team derived from careful thought given to writing and implementing a mission that became the foundation of all the school's work.
5. *Commitment to a mission is much more than philosophical rhetoric—it's hard work.* While common agreement on purpose was essential, the willing-

ness of teachers to design and practice new programs and strategies was at the core of a truly new school design.

6. *Democracy means giving voice to all, and that is a particularly messy process when adolescents are involved.* The modeling of the trust and respect needed to truly nurture democratic values and practices in young people took a great deal of courage, commitment, and time on the part of adults.

7. *When implementing the mission, compromise should only occur where it hurts the least—where it doesn't impact the core beliefs and values. In other words, be selective about your battles.* We knew that the issues of heterogeneity and inclusion would need our strong attention. We chose, therefore, to let go of other possible initiatives to ensure that we would have the energy to win support for this core belief.

8. *The belief that all students can learn can and must be institutionalized into practice.* It is easy to give lip service to such niceties. It was much harder to institute the programs that pushed each student and each teacher to reach those higher standards.

9. *Personalization means more than talking to and caring about some students; it means creating formal structures that ensure all students receive personal care, attention, and support.* Advisory programs, small learning communities (e.g., teams), and individual portfolios were ways for the school to institutionalize personalized practices and not leave personalization to the luck of the draw.

10. *Ongoing communication and strong public relations efforts must keep the community abreast of the change process.* Formal newsletters, seemingly endless meetings, and conscious efforts to meet with as many parents, students, and local citizens as possible made the difference in the community's acceptance of a very new approach to schooling.

11. *Creating a professional learning community requires everyone's attention, commitment, and hard work.* Models for collaborative leadership create and sustain a healthy professional environment; developing multilayers of collaboration requires enormous time, energy, and strong administrative support.

12. *Sustaining new or significantly redesigned school cultures and programs requires an institutionalization of belief systems and practices that will survive when the initial vision-keeper leaves.* Our model of transitional leadership supported Souhegan's future and allowed the culture to take root despite a turnover of administrators. Just as important was our conscious decision to establish a flat leadership design to include dozens of teachers in both formal and informal leadership roles. When many share responsibility for the vision, it acts as a protection that no single leader will be able to dismantle core programs.

AFTERWORD

Souhegan High School remains a dynamic, responsive institution, and so, even as we write our book's final chapter, Souhegan is changing. We have changed some of the student reporting requirements in our Division One Exhibition, we have tinkered with our Senior Project in small ways, and we have a steering committee in place. Scott Prescott and Colleen Meaney have begun their tenure as deans of faculty. Parents, school board members, faculty, administrators, and support staff members are now planning for the future of Souhegan. Although we have passed a bond to build an additional building on our campus, the vote has been challenged in federal court, so we will add another portable classroom and cross our fingers that the delay is a small one.

As in any community, we have shared in wakes and weddings. Since our opening in 1992, we have celebrated two dozen staff weddings and welcomed three dozen new faculty babies, including four babies who arrived within 6 weeks of each other on one tenth-grade team. We have mourned the sudden death of one young teacher, and we are still grieving the loss of Ben Hedges, friend, counselor, and bagpiper. Ben always implored us to avoid "stamping out another teenager at the factory of school." We have supported our colleagues through sickness and loss, and we have attended too many funerals of students. We have also watched with joy as our students march across our graduation stage to find their own life stories. And we continue to ask good questions that speak to the heart of what matters. We take great pride in the observation of the visiting committee of the New England Association of Schools and Colleges (NEASC). In their summary of our initial accreditation process in 1997, they said:

> The visiting team has not seen this type of school in action by so many dedicated people. The greatest compliment to the faculty, the students, and the parents and community is that all members of the visiting committee wish their children could attend Souhegan High School. (p. 4)

In addressing the probability of chaos as we tried a new schedule for Senior Projects, Senior Project coordinator Melanie Gallo urged us to

In all decisions, err in favor of the students.

Hopefully, we will continue to do just that.

Ten Common Principles
of the Coalition
# of Essential Schools

1. The school should focus on helping young people learn to use their minds well. Schools should not be comprehensive if such a claim is made at the expense of the school's central intellectual purpose.
2. The school's goals should be simple: that each student master a limited number of essential skills and areas of knowledge. While these skills and areas will, to varying degrees, reflect the traditional academic disciplines, the program's design should be shaped by the intellectual and imaginative powers and competencies that the students need, rather than by "subjects" as conventionally defined. The aphorism "less is more" should dominate: curricular decisions should be guided by the aim of thorough student mastery and achievement rather than by an effort to merely cover content.
3. The school's goals should apply to all students, while the means to these goals will vary as those students themselves vary. School practice should be tailor-made to meet the needs of every group or class of students.
4. Teaching and learning should be personalized to the maximum feasible extent. Efforts should be directed toward a goal that no teacher have direct responsibility for more than 80 students in the high school and middle school and no more than 20 in the elementary school. To capitalize on this personalization, decisions about the details of the course of study, the use of students' and teachers' time and the choice of teaching materials and specific pedagogies must be unreservedly placed in the hands of the principal and staff.
5. The governing practical metaphor of the school should be student-as-worker, rather than the more familiar metaphor of teacher-as-deliverer-of-instructional-services. Accordingly, a prominent pedagogy will be

coaching, to provoke students to learn how to learn and thus to teach themselves.

6. Teaching and learning should be documented and assessed with tools based on student performance of real tasks. Students not yet at appropriate levels of competence should be provided intensive support and resources to assist them quickly to meet those standards. Multiple forms of evidence, ranging from ongoing observation of the learner to completion of specific projects, should be used to better understand the learner's strengths and needs, and to plan for further assistance. Students should have opportunities to exhibit their expertise before family and community. The diploma should be awarded upon a successful final demonstration of mastery for graduation—an "Exhibition." As the diploma is awarded when earned, the school's program proceeds with no strict age grading and with no system of credits earned by "time spent" in class. The emphasis is on the students' demonstration that they can do important things.

7. The tone of the school should explicitly and self-consciously stress values of unanxious expectation ("I won't threaten you but I expect much of you"), of trust (until abused) and of decency (the values of fairness, generosity, and tolerance). Incentives appropriate to the school's particular students and teachers should be emphasized. Parents should be key collaborators and vital members of the school community.

8. The principal and teachers should perceive themselves as generalists first (teachers and scholars in general education) and specialists second (experts in but one particular discipline). Staff should expect multiple obligations (teacher–counselor–manager) and a sense of commitment to the entire school.

9. Ultimate administrative and budget targets should include, in addition to total student loads per teacher of 80 or fewer pupils on the high school and middle school levels and 20 or fewer on the elementary level, substantial time for collective planning by teachers, competitive salaries for staff, and an ultimate per pupil cost not to exceed that at traditional schools by more than 10 percent. To accomplish this, administrative plans may have to show the phased reduction or elimination of some services now provided students in many traditional schools.

10. The school should demonstrate non-discriminatory and inclusive policies, practices, and pedagogies. It should model democratic practices that involve all who are directly affected by the school. The school should honor diversity and build on the strength of its communities, deliberately and explicitly challenging all forms of inequity.

References

Breaking Ranks: Changing an American Institution. (1996). Reston, VA: National Association of Secondary School Principals.

Covey, S. (1990). *The seven habits of highly successful people.* New York: Simon & Schuster.

Csikszentmihalyi, M. (1996). *Creativity.* New York: HarperCollins.

Darling-Hammond, L. (1997). *The right to learn: A blueprint for creating schools that work.* San Francisco: Jossey-Bass.

Deal, T., & Kennedy, A. (1982). *Corporate cultures.* Reading, MA: Addison-Wesley.

DePree, M. (1992). *Leadership jazz.* New York: Dell.

Fullan, M. (1993). *Change forces: Probing the depth of education reform.* London: Falmer.

Fullan, M., & Hargreaves, A. (1996). *What's worth fighting for in your school.* New York: Teachers College Press.

Glickman, C. (1993). *Renewing America's schools.* San Francisco: Jossey-Bass.

Kennedy, M. (Ed.). (1998). *Make gentle the life of the world: The vision of Robert F. Kennedy.* New York: Harcourt Brace.

Kruse, S., & Louis, K. S. (1995). *Brief to principals No. 11.* Madison, WI: Center on Organization and Restructuring of Schools.

Little, J. W., & McLaughlin, M. (Eds.) (1993). *Teacher's work: Individuals, colleagues, and contexts.* New York: Teachers College Press.

Mackin, R. (1996, December). "Hey, Dr. Bob, can we talk?": Toward the creation of a personalized high school. *NASSP Bulletin* (pp. 9–16). Reston, VA: National Association of Secondary School Principals.

Marzano, R. (1994). Unpublished conference materials. Littleton, CO: Mid-Continent Research for Education and Learning.

Meier, D. (2000). *Will standards save public education?* Boston: Beacon Press.

New England Association of Schools and Colleges. (1997). Report of the visiting committee. Paula Schwartz, Chair; Edward Higgins, Assistant Chair; Patrick Schettini, Assistant Chair.

Oldfield, D. (1987). *The journey: A creative approach to the necessary crises of adolescence.* Washington, DC: David Oldfield and the Foundation for Contemporary Mental Health.

Pado, T. (1995). *The Division One Exhibition.* Unpublished master's thesis, University of New Hampshire, Durham.

Reich, R. (2001, June 20). Standards for what? *Education Week*, p. 48.

Senge, P. (1990). *The fifth discipline: The art and practice of the learning organization.* New York: Doubleday.

Sizer, T. (1984). *Horace's compromise: The dilemma of the American high school.* Boston: Houghton Mifflin.

Sizer, T. (1992). *Horace's school: Redesigning the American high school.* Boston: Houghton-Mifflin.

West, C. (2000, November). Opening remarks made at the opening session of the Coalition of Essential Schools fall forum 2000, Providence, RI.

Index

About the Authors

Peggy Silva. Prior to becoming a charter member of the faculty of Souhegan High School, Peggy served as a volunteer member of the Curriculum Committee, helping to develop the philosophy of this new school. Peggy taught for several years in Nashua and Hollis, New Hampshire, then earned an MBA degree and worked in sales, marketing, and staff development. Challenged by the superintendent of schools to join in planning the ideal learning environment for students and teachers, she returned to secondary education. She has team-taught humanities as a member of a ninth-grade team at Souhegan High School since 1992. She is also a member of the National School Reform Faculty.

Peggy has written several articles for the Writing Within School Reform series of the Annenberg Institute for School Reform. She is a founding member of Educators Writing for Change and is a co-author of *Reflection: The Heart of Changing Practice*. Peggy and her husband, John, have lived in Amherst, New Hampshire, for more than 25 years. They have two daughters, Meghan and Kerry. Peggy can be reached at Peggysilva1@earthlink.net.

Robert A. Mackin. Before becoming the founding principal of Souhegan High School, Bob Mackin served as principal of both the Fox Lane Middle School and Fox Lane High School in Bedford, New York. Fox Lane High School was an early member of the Coalition of Essential Schools. During his tenure at Souhegan, the high school was selected as the outstanding high school in New Hampshire in 1994 and as a *Redbook* magazine "Best School" in 1996.

Bob was the 1995 New Hampshire Principal of the Year and was runner-up for the National High School Principal of the Year award in 1996. He is a member of the National School Reform Faculty, formerly of the Annenberg Institute of School Reform at Brown University, and recently served as director of Breaking Ranks in the Ocean State at Brown University. In 1998, as a member of the Commission on Public Secondary Schools of the New England Association of Schools and Colleges [NEASC], he led the rewriting of accreditation standards in New England. A workshop leader and keynote speaker for more than 25 years, Bob currently serves as president of LEAD New England, an educational consulting firm that supports high school redesign throughout New England.

Bob grew up and graduated from high school in Norwalk, Connecticut. He received his BA in politics, cum laude, from Princeton University, his MA in education from Stanford University, and his EdD in administration and school reform from the University of Massachusetts, Amherst. He presently resides in New Hampshire with his wife, Eileen, a practicing visual artist and an arts-in-education specialist. Bob's e-mail address is LeadNE@aol.com.